Kumamoto Sojourn

Kumamoto Sojourn

Leslee Inaba Wong

iUniverse, Inc.
New York Lincoln Shanghai

Kumamoto Sojourn

Copyright © 2005 by Leslee Inaba Wong

iUniverse books may be ordered through booksellers or by contacting:

iUniverse
2021 Pine Lake Road, Suite 100
Lincoln, NE 68512
www.iuniverse.com
1-800-Authors (1-800-288-4677)

ISBN-13: 978-0-595-37496-0 (pbk)
ISBN-13: 978-0-595-81889-1 (ebk)
ISBN-10: 0-595-37496-4 (pbk)
ISBN-10: 0-595-81889-7 (ebk)

Printed in the United States of America

TO MOM AND IN MEMORY, DAD

Acknowledgements

I humbly thank my family: GT for his many hours of careful editing and loving support; Asia for her insightful suggestions and comments; and Kumiko for working over my fractured Japanese. And my gratitude to the loving memory of Ila Nehre, friend and copy editor of early versions.

Preface

Ten women traveled to Japan together in the summer of 1997. Ten bodies: ten pair of eyes, ears, and hands; ten noses and mouths; ten different takes.

I can already hear the chorus of voices protesting, "It did not happen that way!" From my fellow travelers, I seek indulgence. We were all on that tour, but this is my journey. And where pure fabrication is detected, I plead the right to artistic license.

INTRODUCTION

The way my mother tells it, she promised one of her granddaughters she would take her to Japan. That promise snowballed into a minor avalanche and in late June of 1997, there was my slightly bewildered mother, wondering how it came to pass she was taking me and my daughter, my sisters and sisters-in-law, and nieces on a two week tour of Japan.

What happened to the men in our families? We left them behind. The exclusion was not intended as any type of political statement (my mother was a generation away from the feminist movement), but was simply the result of how the trip unfolded, and our journey was an experience without testosterone.

I was also traveling for the first time as a diabetic (having been diagnosed shortly before our trip commenced) and was still learning to manage the roller coaster rides that resulted from my body's unstable sugar levels.

From June 18 through July 1 of 1997, we—Grandma, moms, aunties, sisters, sisters-in-law, daughters, nieces, and cousins—ten women shared an unforgettable journey in the land of our ancestry.

Monday, 16th of June 1997
New York to San Francisco

It was my habit to take goodies from New York to California, and I had become an expert at transporting everything from smoked whitefish to baked sugary palm leaves coast to coast. This trip out—despite the protest of my husband GT—I had two cheesecakes stored in the overhead luggage bin of our airplane.

GT, our daughter Asia, and I had taken off from Kennedy Airport bound for San Francisco. Six months earlier, I had a phone call from my mother. "Before Dad died, we promised Asia that we would take her to Japan," she explained. My father had passed away four years earlier, and she felt she was ready to make good her promise. "I was thinking that if I take Asia, I should take Cindy too. But if I take them, I have to take Stephanie and Robyn." By a short extension, she absorbed all of her granddaughters into her initial promise. "But what was I going to do with four young girls? So I thought I would take their mothers, that's you and Diane and Judy. And if I did that, I have two other daughters Sharon and Lynne and they might as well go too." And there she drew the line.

San Francisco was the designated point of origin for our trip. Asia and I planned to spend a day there before embarking with the rest of our tour group to Tokyo. GT would see us off and then spend a week vacationing on the West Coast. I was glad he was doing that. He was good-natured about his wife and daughter abandoning him for two weeks, but leaving him in hot, sticky New York City while Asia and I jetted off to Japan seemed too sad.

Our flight was full-to-capacity, and I was worried about the cheesecakes. As much as GT fussed about it, the Japanese custom of giving *omiyage* or gifts to one's hosts was so totally programmed into my travel practices that I could no more appear in San Francisco without something for my relatives than leave an arm or leg at home. Luckily our flight went smoothly, and we all managed to make it to San Francisco in good condition, cheesecakes in tow.

We collected our baggage and headed to my brother Darryl's house. His wife Diane and I would be roommates for the Japan tour. Our families had vacationed together and Diane was a fun sidekick. She also had a particular talent, a heightened sense of smell. She could detect odors from long distances and analyze their contents (as in, *ten percent cigarette smoke, twenty percent aftershave, and the rest B.O.)* A talent that carried advantages and obvious disadvantages.

Darryl and Diane lived near the San Francisco Zoo and within walking distance to the ocean. We pulled up in front of their driveway and Asia bounded up the front steps eager to meet up with her cousins. My daughter was a thoroughly New York City kid, raised in the Lower East Side and attired in urban grunge. Her cousin Cynthia (or Cindy or Cyn) presented more conventionally, but had a playful quality that engaged whenever she and Asia were together. Despite living on opposite coasts and seeing each other only about once a year, Asia and Cindy got along well and had great fun together.

Diane greeted us and I took the New York cheesecakes and headed for the kitchen. The family's fat Siamese cat, Nibbles, scampered across the kitchen floor and into the hallway. Perhaps scampered is not the right word, because he had a huge tumor in his belly that slowed him down, made him appear as though he were pregnant, and tilted him over to one side whenever he moved.

Faced with the task of buying *omiyage* for the scores of friends and relatives who had been notified of our impending visit, my sister Lynne, Diane, and I collaborated on a plan to pool our resources and give gifts jointly. Toward that end, we had been shopping for months and our agenda for the day was to sort, wrap, and tag gifts.

Lynne drove up from Fresno and brought lots of extra *omiyage*. Anyone who had ever shopped with my younger sister knew she was used to buying anything that caught her fancy. She was generous by nature, and since *omiyage* traveled two ways, was sure to purchase many presents to bring back as well. She would probably need them, since she was leaving at home her husband Bob and three sons, and lots of low level grumbling about the gender exclusiveness of our group.

We displayed our purchases in Diane's dining room, and her table looked like it was the week before Christmas. We had enough *omiyage* to fill two suitcases. Surely with all extras we were taking, we could give gifts to the whole of Japan!

Giggles spilled out of Cindy's room. She and Asia were hitting their stride. Stephanie, Diane's youngest daughter came sauntering into the dining room. Whenever Asia and Cindy got together, Steph was the odd person out and often ended up hanging around the adults. "What's this?" she asked looking over our loot. "*Omiyage* for Japan. You want to help us wrap?" I suggested. "I'm not good at this, but okay," she volunteered with good humor.

Darryl came home just as we were packing the last gift. My brother loved bits of family gossip and I was sorry that I did not have anything to share, especially since he had uncharacteristically left work early. In the late 1960's Darryl began working at the Haight-Ashbury Free Medical Clinic. He was an intern in pharmacy school, and the Clinic operated out of a rented flat in the center of San Francisco's hippiedom. He was still working there thirty years later. Like so many serve-the-people kinds of non-profit programs, the Clinic was in perpetual crisis, and Darryl was on twenty-four hour call. Even when he came east to vacation with us, he called into work and put out brush fires. I suspected that while we were in Japan, he would be too busy to miss his wife and daughters during the day, although his nights would undoubtedly be lonely.

I collected my New York cheesecakes and we all went to my youngest brother Don's house for dinner. A few weeks earlier Don's fiancée Kumiko had finally cleared bureaucratic hurdles and emigrated from Kobe, Japan. Their wedding day was set for later that summer.

Kumiko and Don met while she was an exchange teacher in a grade school attended by one of my nephews. If I had personally screened every woman in the universe, I do not think I could find one more suited to my brother. They both shared an artistic bent. Both had a great sense of humor. Both were at the age where they could appreciate the genuine goodness in each other. The first time I saw Don and Kumiko together, I had the sensation that they were two souls that had traveled many past lifetimes together.

Kumiko was leaving her mother and sister in Kobe to marry my brother. I was afraid that she would get homesick, but when I inquired she said she was not. Since she was just settling in, she would not be traveling with the rest of us Inaba women. Her influence in Don's life was already evident. My little brother's house was becoming domesticated. All of the mismatched things he inherited like my parents' old Formica covered table had taken on a feminine look with little decorative plants and knick-knacks. The crowning touch was Don's elaborate collection of plastic Tupperware and margarine containers. Kumiko had organized an entire drawer, marking the tops to match the containers. If that was any indication of her organizational abilities, she would have Don wearing matching socks in no time.

Kumiko had prepared lots of food Japanese-style: bits of everything from soup to nuts. Don took the *obento*, the lunches she packed to show off at the office. His jealous co-workers hated him. She and Don made the perfect hosts. It was Darryl's birthday, and we toasted him with champagne. We toasted Kumiko's welcome into the family, and our bon voyage; and ended the festivities with cheesecake for dessert.

For going away presents Don and Kumiko gave each of us an origami paper kimono in which they had inserted a two-thousand-yen note. Life does not get much better. Although as the evening wound down, Asia appeared to be a little under the weather.

Tuesday, 17th of June and Wednesday, 18th of June 1997
San Francisco to Tokyo: Keio Plaza Hotel

We were scheduled to leave San Francisco on June 17th at one o'clock in the afternoon Pacific Daylight Saving Time, and arrive in Tokyo on June 18th at three-forty in the afternoon Tokyo time the next day. I was trying to calculate all of the times by Eastern Daylight Saving Time because that was the time zone to which my body was most accustomed, and was having a hard time. Like today, if we left San Francisco at one o'clock in the afternoon, it would be four o'clock in New York, because of the three-hour time difference. Okay, that was easy enough. Then we got to Tokyo at three-forty in the afternoon, Tokyo time. Now that should be five-forty in the morning in New York, because New York was fourteen hours behind Tokyo. But how could that be if San Francisco was three hours behind New York? I was sure it had to do with crossing some international date line, but I could not untangle the logic. Where was Einstein when I needed him?

I got up still functioning on New York time, anxious to exercise because I anticipated being cooped up for many hours on the airplane. I dressed and went out for a jog on the beach and along the Great Highway. The day was overcast with low hanging fog and lots of mist. The official start of summer was four days away, but the weather pattern typical of San Francisco summers had already settled into the coast. The scent of eucalyptus permeated the air. It was such a Bay Area aroma, full of hippy lifestyle associations.

This was one of my favorite jogging paths; cars zoomed along the Great Highway on the east, and the Pacific Ocean expanded on the west. I had run along this same ocean in Hermosa Beach four hundred miles to the south. I was staying with my friend Elizabeth and ran along the seashore on a promenade that curved next to low beach bungalows. There was more beach down there, and more sun, and girls in bikinis. No bikini clad girls romped along this stretch of beach. On the rocky coast below, a woman sporting a pea coat and blue jeans walked a shaggy dog. Everyone on this beach was wearing a jacket or sweatshirt.

Forty-eight hours ago and three-thousand miles away, I was running on the esplanade next to the East River. Across a narrow strip of parkland to the west, cars hissed along on the FDR Drive. The East River feeds into the Atlantic Ocean about a mile downstream, and I could see the Statue of Liberty.

No waves broke onto the shores of the East River, but the waves incessantly crashed along this rocky part of the Pacific Ocean. There was no marker, no Statue of Liberty, visible from this shore. Only the vast horizon, beyond which I knew were islands and other continents. In a matter of hours I would be landing on one of those unseen islands. I had never been more aware of how tightly the world was pulled together than at that moment ready to embark on my journey. In seventy-two hours, I would have done what it took months to complete a little more than a century ago.

I reached the end of my run and started my cool-down power-walk back to Diane's house. Somewhere along the way, I took a wrong turn and each time I came to an intersection, it was not the one I expected. I got small charges of panic. It was so easy to find the house, I told myself. Could it be early Alzheimer's???

I finally reached 19th Avenue, a recognizable intersection. I walked about four-fifths of a mile back to Diane's house and when I finally got there, she was a bit concerned knowing that I had been gone too long.

My sister Sharon's house was the rendezvous point for our touring group. Sharon and her husband Dan had just moved into a new house and she was eager to show it off. Sharon met Dan when she was in pharmacy school. He was handsome and dashing and swept her off her feet. They married and moved into a small apartment near the mouth of a streetcar tunnel; then moved three times after that, each time to a better home. This latest move was into a model house in the outer Mission District, and since I had never been there, Sharon insisted it be the meeting place for our group.

Sharon could do that. She was the eldest in our family and used to calling the shots. My mother and father had both worked when we were growing up and Sharon had often been in charge of taking care of her five younger siblings, second in command only to my Grandmother Hamaoka who lived with us.

We were the last group to arrive at Sharon's house. It was a lovely home built in three split-levels, but I was too jazzed about our trip to give it much attention. Mom was waiting for us when we got there. She rode down from Sacramento with my brother Harley, his wife Judy, and their daughter Robyn. When Harley showed an interest in the family import business, my father sent him to Japan to learn the ropes from that end. Judy and their three children who were at that time all under the age of four joined him, and they lived in Japan for over a year. Judy's familiarity with the cadence of Japan would help us stay on track and on schedule. If Mom was the general of our troops, Judy was the sergeant.

Our room assignments could not have been more perfect. Mom and Sharon would be roommates. I was with Diane, and Asia with Cindy. Judy was paired up with Lynne; they had been best friends in high school. Stephanie and Robyn the teenagers in our group, ages nineteen and eighteen respectively, would be bunking together.

Mom had made bright pink five-inch yarn pom-poms to fix onto our luggage so that they would be easy to spot. Our luggage tags identified us as a Sacramento tour group. We generated a great feeling of anticipation about to begin a wonderful adventure. Harley looked happy for us, and Mom was excited.

Then the pushing and pulling started. We were getting into cars to go to the airport. "You go in this car," Sharon bossed. "And they go in that car." "Just back off," I bossed back. Lynne guffawed aloud. Diane rolled her eyes. Judy jumped into her van. Mom said, "See? *Mata, mo,*" which roughly translated means, "You two are at it again!" Then threw us *the look* (as she had throughout our childhoods) that made us stop fussing.

At the airport we lined up for group pictures, all ten of us. It was the first of about a hundred such photographs we would take over the next two weeks. We kissed our husbands, the girls kissed their fathers, and we boarded the plane. We were flying Japan Air Lines, sitting in the upper cabin courtesy of a family friend who worked for the airline.

Our excitement carried us for about four hours. Then Diane (who really does not like to fly) got a little nervous. Asia was sick, fighting off some kind of bug. I was restless and got up to walk around, but there were only so many places to go. Finally, the stewardesses gave instructions for landing. I had some dried apricots and an apple to help manage my diabetic sugar drops, but fruit was on a "Cannot Bring Into Japan" list and being overly cautious, I left them in the airplane.

Waiting in line at Customs, we were rumpled and tired, but excited. We were in Japan! Diane was standing next to me. She sniffed the air and declared, "This smells like Japan." I knew I would be rooming with the sniff-sniff police for the next two weeks, but she was right. I remember as a child opening boxes tied with paper string, knowing by the musty, woody, fishy odor that the package came from Japan.

"*Ka-san!*" a familiar voice called out. Hisakazu Iwata stood behind a barrier and waved. Next to him were his wife Hajime, and brother Katsuyuki, and sister-in-law Junko. They had come to greet us and escort us to our hotel.

Mom met Hisakazu when he was touring America with the Japanese National Judo team; and his addressing Mom as "*Ka-san*" or mother, indicated how close they had become. The previous year Hisakazu had been in San Francisco for major surgery. He and Hajime had stayed with Sharon, and my family had helped navigate him through the confusing and often stormy seas of American medical care. Hisakazu and Hajime (and by extension their entire families) were grateful for our family's help, and when they learned of our visit, they pulled out all stops. For the next two weeks, they would step in to fill the gaps in our tour, entertaining us when we had a free day and carting us about. We would learn that Japanese hospitality knows very few bounds.

Hisakazu took the lead, helped us collect our luggage, and headed us toward the curb to board the bus for our hotel. The sky was gray, and the air heavily humid. Standing on the curbside, we were surrounded by the ambience of Japan.

> *Black bags, pink pom-poms.*
> *Sticky Narita Airport.*
> *Inaba girls land!*

Intending to get my first look at Japan, I sat next to the window on the bus, but I kept dozing off. After all, according to my watch, I was pretty much standing on my head in terms of New York time; that is, expected to be awake when I should have been sleeping.

The bus drove into downtown Tokyo and after a couple of stops, pulled into the driveway of the Keio Plaza Hotel, a modern-high rise that could have been in the heart of New York City or San Francisco or Hong Kong for that matter. If it was any indication of our lodgings to come, we would be going "Four Stars" all the way.

We checked in and deposited our bags in our rooms. I was ready for bed, but the group plan was to get something to eat. We followed Hisakazu and Katsuyuki into the streets of Tokyo, and up to a food court in some big "Trump Towers" kind of building. We were very, very tired and elected to eat at a noodle shop that (as my roommate pointed out) had sticky tables and a sticky floor.

Back at the hotel, Asia was under the weather but I knew despite how badly she felt she would resist whatever virus coming on. She would not want to miss one second of Japan. Luckily, Diane had brought along the entire contents of a pharmacy. We gave Asia an antibiotic, and then crashed out for the night.

Thursday, 19th of June 1997
Tokyo: Meiji Shrine/ Tokyo Tower/ Nakamise Shopping Arcade

Our first full day in Japan. I was eager to get out. Diane lay like a lump in her bed. We were due to meet our guide Ken Suzuki at nine o'clock. I needed coffee and some kind of breakfast with which to take my diabetes meds. I consulted the hotel map and found that we were in the Shinjuku area of Tokyo, close to the Tokyo Medical College Hospital, Tokyo City Hall, and the Tokyo Metropolitan Assembly. From our window, I could see a wide boulevard running next to the hotel. Two cars rode along the boulevard, and there were no pedestrians on the sidewalks. An official building stood across the street, which I learned later was a post office. It was five-minutes-past-six in the morning, Tokyo time. If it were downtown Manhattan, the streets would be awakening with commuter traffic. The sky was overcast, and it was the start of a hot, humid day.

I left Diane sleeping and hit the streets. On the sidewalk ahead of me was a group of five middle-aged women. Three of them were in kimono, and the other two were dressed in dark skirts and white blouses. They gaily chatted away. I had taken a crash course in conversational Japanese as preparation for this trip, and inched up closer to them hoping to listen in on their dialogue. But they were speaking too rapidly and I could not catch individual words. They reached the end of the block and a traffic light blinked to green and sang, "Ding-ding." One of the women sang, "Ding-ding," back and they all giggled. "Ding-ding" I understood.

Across the street through a narrow alley, a row of vending machines beckoned. Maybe coffee? Packaged Danish? A long shot, but worth a try. The hotel was behind me and plainly visible. I crossed the street and charted my course according to it, since I could not afford to get lost as I had in San Francisco.

The vending machines issued cold beverages: *Cha*, bottled water, *Calpis* (a popular Japanese soft drink), and beer. No luck there. But I had been lured into an area of low buildings with pagoda style peaked roofs. Small shops lined a pedestrian pathway paved with stones. The whole area took up about one square city block.

The ravens cried out announcing their presence before I spotted them. A rowdy bunch of birds that perched on top of the rafters and swept down to peck through garbage. As obnoxious as New York pigeons, though not nearly so tame.

"Caw, caw!" Raven wings
Slapping sultry air. Shop-lined
Narrow street, Tokyo.

I felt as though I was on a movie set about early modern Japan. This small square sat in a valley of high-rise modern commercial and government buildings that surrounded it, as though it was its own village. There must be hundreds of squares like this throughout Tokyo.

Pictures of *udon* and *donburi,* noodle and rice dishes, hung from some of the shop windows. One of the shops had a Dutch-style double door with the top part open. I walked up and looked into a long, narrow room with a counter running along one side. Sitting on a high stool in front of the counter was a man in a business suit. He was slurping noodles from a deep *udon* bowl. A woman wearing a brown kerchief over her hair and a blue apron over her clothes stood behind the counter. From the back of the shop, where there must have been a kitchen, wafted the scent of *dashi,* the fish broth that is the base of all soup and noodle dishes.

I opened the door, took a deep breath, stepped into the shop, and go for what I know. "Can I order this to go?" I asked in my best English. The woman looked at me. Blank. The man stopped slurping from his bowl and held his chopsticks midair. It is not true what they say. Not everyone in Tokyo speaks English. I had to go for what I did not know.

"A-no ne, ko-no ta-bé mo-nó wa, wa-ta-shi no hó-te-ru ni…", which roughly translated to, "This foodstuff, to my hotel…?" *"Ā,"* answered the woman behind the counter, her face lighting up. *"Teuku autou?"* *"Hai!"* Yes! Take out! *"Teuku autou!"* We both smiled and nodded, happy that we connected. I could envision all the containers of noodles that I would take with me back to the hotel. Everyone would be so happy!

"Inai," she said, shaking her head. "No?" I asked. She shook her head again. I hardly believed her. After all of our efforts, she was telling me, "No." I shook my head and walked backwards through the front door. I did not even say *"Arígatō."* Maybe she would think I was an ill-mannered Korean rather than an illiterate sansei.

I walked so that the hotel was to my right. In the front of a modern bakery/coffee shop, a young man wearing scruffy jeans and a gray T-shirt was putting up a sandwich board sign. I approached him.

"Are you open?" I asked. He looked up at me. "Yea," he said in impeccable English. Hot dog! The *kissaten,* the bakery/coffee shop, sold everything I was looking for and more. I bought six cups of coffee, assorted pastries, and sandwiches with the crust cut off. The girl behind the counter was at times a little bewildered, but managed to get my order right.

"How late are you open?" I asked the counter girl. She looked at me like "What?" Like "Que?" The young man I met before came over. "Six o'clock," he answered. I thanked him. I was happy. I had been successful with my first attempts at communication in Japan. Mom had not wasted her money paying for my childhood Japanese language lessons after all.

I took my loot to share with my nine sister travelers. Asia said she felt a little better and I could see that the antibiotic was having an effect. But her eyes were still puffy and it was clear she was not entirely well.

Ken Suzuki, our tour guide, was waiting in the driveway of the hotel. He appeared to be in his late fifties and wore glasses, a light tan jacket, and khaki slacks. He stood next to a van with "Inaba Family" printed on a paper banner taped to the top of the windshield. We handed Ken our cameras and he took the same picture of us standing in front of the van with ten different cameras. We took the banner (as we would from our private tour vans for the next several days) and climbed aboard.

"Who wants to sit in the front with me?" Ken asked. No one immediately answered. I waited a courteous five seconds, then volunteered, "I will!" New York trained me well. Any frequent bus rider knows that the best view is from the front seat. I sat in the seat across from Mr. Suzuki. His English was perfect. He informed me that he was retired and did this tour guide thing on the side. I asked if he had lived in the U.S. He said "No," but his English usage and understanding made me think that he must have spent some time in the States.

The van driver signaled left, and turned onto to a wide boulevard. Instinctively I lurched forward in my seat, wanting to stop the driver from moving into what I thought would be head-on traffic. Then I remembered that in Japan vehicles drive on the opposite side of the street from the U.S. I relaxed for the rest of the ride.

Our first stop, the Meiji Shrine!

We rounded a corner and drove towards a big wooden gateway that opened up to the grounds of the Meiji Shrine. The grounds were lush with plants and trees. The wooden gate, Mr. Suzuki said, was a *torii* gate. It was constructed with two log pillars connected across the top with two wooden planks. The shape of the top crosspiece swept upwards, like the wings of a bird, hence the name *torii*.

Carved into the top crossbar was the official seal of the Royal Family, a chrysanthemum with twelve petals set in a circle. Mr. Suzuki informed us that in order to be the authentic crest, the flower *must* have twelve petals.

We disembarked from the van in the parking lot. Two steps led up to a pathway onto the grounds. Judy called out, "Look!" and pointed to a sign that read, "Watch Your Foot." The opportunity was too choice to pass up, and she kicked up her leg as we took pictures of her watching her foot.

The air was thick and damp, the harbinger of a storm to come. We walked through the grounds and came onto the shrine. At its entrance stood an open structure with a roof that covered a water trough or *chozuya*. Fresh water flowed into the trough, and wooden cups with long handles sat on a shelf next to it. Ken taught us how to wash our hands and rinse our mouths, a way of cleansing ourselves before we entered the shrine. A table with Meiji Shrine rubber stamps stood next to the *chozuya*. We lined up to stamp our books, as we would at every site we visited for the rest of our tour.

Next to the stamp table were freestanding wooden frames about five feet tall. Bits of paper tied to strings hung from the crossbars and twisted in the breeze like tails of kites. "This is where students come to pray for good grades before their major examinations." Ken explained. "They write down their wishes, and tie them to the strings."

> *A sighting of an image of the Virgin Mary occurred a block away from the hospital where I work in New York City. A piece of scaffolding from a building came down and split a limb off a tree. According to the citizens of the neighborhood, an image of the Madonna appeared on the exposed part of the trunk. Spontaneously, a shrine was created. Pilgrims came from miles around to pray at the holy place. Candles and flowers adorned the base of the tree. Rosaries hung from the tree's branches. Prayers written on pieces of paper were posted with pushpins and tape onto its trunk. Someone had written, "Deliver my son from the evils of drugs." Another prayed for healing from cancer. No one asked for high scores on the SATs. Education in Japan is a serious business.*

Ken led us onto a raised wood plank walkway. We followed him about fifty yards, made a sharp ninety-degree turn, and crossed in front of a platform that was open on the sides, walled in the back, and covered with an impressive copper roof. The roof was supported by log pillars. The back wall painted white. This was it. The shrine. Minimalist.

Jeopardy category: Places of worship
Answer: The opposite of a Gothic cathedral.
Question: What is a Shinto shrine?

Ken explained that Shintoism was a religion that emphasized the interconnection of all things and their inherent connection to nature. Thus, all of the shrines opened up to and were integrated into their natural surroundings. I looked back toward the entrance to the shrine. Sure enough, there was a clearly defined open oblong area, like the middle in a block **U**. Raised wooden walkways defined the side perimeters of the area and the white-walled structure defined its end.

We followed Ken across the front of the platform, then away from it on the raised walkway opposite from and parallel to the one on which we had entered. Then we followed Ken out of the shrine and into the surrounding grounds.

The grounds were lovely, green, and rolling. We walked along footpaths next to well-kept grass. Mr. Ken Suzuki pointed to a teahouse. (Mom and Dad had a teahouse built in our backyard in Fresno, but of course, this one was fancier.) "That was where the Emperor's consort took her tea," he explained.

"What's a consort, Auntie?" Stephanie asked. "His mistress," I answered, not really knowing myself, but thinking the Japanese were pretty sophisticated.

Souvenir stands dotted the footpaths at regular intervals. We stopped at every one of them, looked, and bought.

Mr. Suzuki walked us to a garden and announced that irises were on show. At a wooden gate we grownups made the girls squat in front of some flowering potted irises so that we could take pictures.

Stepping through the gate, we found ourselves at one end of a winding brook. Irises were clustered in every crook and bend in the brook and all along its banks.

The irises were in bloom.

> *Purple hues washed gray.*
> *Irises bloom in winding*
> *Creek on Meiji grounds.*

Small footbridges crisscrossed the brook. Along the banks were artists with their easels, photographers with their cameras, school children in their white tops and dark bottoms, and tourists like us.

We meandered down a path next to the brook, then followed Ken out of the garden into the parking lot. We were about to head towards our van when we spotted the entrance to a gift shop. Lynne and I went in first, and then the others followed. We spent a good half-hour there. I think that is when Ken Suzuki first realized that he had lost us. We were not going to be a well-behaved regular tourist group from the States. We were shopping!

We found some typically tourist-type merchandise: water colors of irises painted on fans, colorful confectionaries, small decorative plates. Lynne and I took our treasures to a cashier. He totaled up the goods and announced the amount very rapidly in Japanese. I began to count on my fingers, *"Ichi–en, ni–en, san–en…"* or one dollar, two dollars, three dollars…. Lynne elbowed me out of the way. "Here," she said and thrust her wallet at the clerk. The clerk was startled. Then he said, *"Ma, kono obasan wa kanemōchi!"* or "What a rich old lady." He then pointed to a five-thousand yen note, and Lynne pulled it out and paid for the goods.

We finally re-boarded the van and went on to the Tokyo Tower…ho hum. Not to be snotty, but I have been to the top of the Empire State Building. As a group, we preferred ground activities.

We hit the jackpot at our next stop, the Nakamise Shopping Arcade. A big wooden gate opened to a narrow walkway. At the end of the pathway was a huge pagoda-shaped open-air altar on which sat a statue of the Buddha. It was the Asakusa Kannon Temple. In front of the temple, on the two sides of the Buddha, were big iron pots holding sticks of burning incense. People stood around these stations, lit more sticks of incense, and prayed. Smoke from the burning incense swilled above the cauldrons and soaked the air with the scent of sandalwood.

A woman wearing a light tan jacket and dark blue skirt stood close to one of the pots and waved the vapors from the burning incense over her head, cupping her hands as though she could catch the smoke and pour it over her body. I guessed the vapors were thought to have some healing powers. I think the Japanese are every bit as superstitious as the Chinese, only we do not have as many gods and goddesses.

There were small commercial stalls and booths set up in three parallel rows leading from the temple to the gate. Consulting our itinerary I learned that we were in the Nakamise Shopping Arcade. I imagine there must be centers like Nakamise in cities all around the world; places where, in feudal times, merchants came to sell their goods. Although these centers grew as the city evolved, they basically remained the same. Think of an outdoor bazaar selling "All Things Japanese," and you have the Nakamise marketplace.

Ken tried to get us into the temple so that he could give his tour guide talk. We gave him the equivalent of "Yeah, yeah, yeah…" Lynne spoke out. "We want to shop." "Shop?" he asked. We all nodded our heads. He shook his. "Okay, come back here in ten minutes." "Ten minutes?" Lynne asked in a tone of voice that suggested he was deranged. "We need at least an hour." "Twenty minutes," Ken countered. We agreed. We were not going to waste more time bartering minutes any longer. Lynne walked away muttering, "Ten minutes. He must be crazy!"

We twisted through the shops, comfortable in our element. I glanced over the merchandise: trinkets, obi and kimono material. One booth displayed an assortment of folding fans. Some were very lovely, but nothing I wanted to purchase.

Small statues of the Buddha were set in little alcoves near the temple, positioned like the Stations of the Cross in Catholic cathedrals. I was done looking, but the others were not. Killing time, I told Asia to stand near one of the small shrines so that I could take a picture. Even when she was feeling well, having her picture taken was not one of her favorite things. A look that could kill is what she threw my way.

Ken loaded us back into the van, and we headed for our last stop of the day, the Imperial Palace grounds. Ken informed us that the palace was surrounded by many gardens and a moat.

Lynne said, "Is it man-made?" Ken said, "What?" It was late in the day, and we were all tired. I thought maybe I had misheard Lynne's question. "The moat. Is it man-made?" Lynne asked again. From the back of the van came sounds of muffled sniggering. Someone said, "Of course it is. That's the definition of a moat." And we all joined in, knocking Lynne about for a while. Except Ken. I do not think he ever got the question.

We were not allowed to walk on the palace grounds, but could walk in the gardens around them. The driver circled the parking lot, which was almost empty, and pulled to a stop. "I've seen it," Mom said. "No need to get off." "You don't want to get out?" Ken asked. "No. That's enough." Mom answered. Ken shrugged his shoulders. He knew it useless to try to persuade us. We all headed back to the hotel with our bewildered van driver and frustrated tour guide.

That night the Iwatas came to our hotel to take us out to dinner. Hisakazu, Hajime and their three children and nephew; Katsuyuki and Junko and their two sons; plus our group made twenty for dinner. Reservations were made in a fancy restaurant high above Tokyo. I was in the elevator with Hajime, Junko, and Chie—Hajime's thirteen-year-old daughter. Prodded by her mother and aunt to speak to me, she looked at the floor and said, "Is New York dangerous?" in perfect English. I was so happy someone was asking me something in English, that I quickly answered, "No, it's not dangerous." End of conversation. I wished I could say more in Japanese. I would have told her about the city and the streets and Central Park and all of the things I love, but I was linguistically challenged. I could only imagine how long it took her to formulate her question.

The elevator doors opened, and we were ushered into a private room with four western-style tables and a view of the city. Hisakazu had mixed it up so that his older children and nephew could sit with our girls to practice their English. Rika, who was the baby of the bunch, wanted to sit next to her cousin and started to complain. Hisakazu gave her a stern look and said, "Rika." That's all, just her name. And she stopped. Lynne laughed and said, "It's the same all over. One word from the dad, and it's over."

It was our first meal with a Japanese family. Conversationally, it was a challenge. "It's like this," Asia described to me later. "There is this long silence as everyone tries to figure out how to say something in whatever language they want to say it. Then someone says, 'Do you go to school?' Then we say, 'Yes.' Then there is another long pause. But we all tried very hard."

I was jet lagged and tumbled into bed. I probably snored out my roommate, although Diane claimed, having slept with Darryl for years, she was used to it.

Friday, 20ᵗʰ of June 1997
Tokyo to Hakone: Mt. Fuji

We awoke to a CNN broadcast predicting a typhoon headed our way. I was out early and bought more sandwiches and coffee from the bakery. Our itinerary for the day listed a full schedule of activities around Mt. Fuji. We were booked to take a cruise, more like a boat ride, on Lake Ashi near Hakone where we would spend the night. By eight o'clock, we were assembled in the lobby. Mr. Suzuki met and informed us that because of the impending storm, the cruise was cancelled. We could drive up to Mt. Fuji, but would not be able to get beyond the Visitor Center. We were on holiday! A little typhoon was not going to faze us. We got into a new van with a new driver. The sky was dark, and it began to rain.

As we traveled south on a modern four-lane highway, the sky grew darker and the rain fell harder until it was coming down in torrents. By the time we reached the city at the base of the mountain, water flooded into the streets and poured down inclines like big streams. We were in the midst of Typhoon Opal.

Our van stopped in front of a modern building with plate glass windows and doors. Eleven umbrellas flipped open; eleven bodies scurried in. The Visitor Center at Mt. Fuji was like those in National Parks throughout the U.S. It contained a reception desk and racks of literature; a plaster scale-model of the mountain; small theater; and refreshment stand where souvenirs were also sold.

Mr. Suzuki conferred with workers behind the desk, who confirmed that all the paths up the mountain were closed. We were free to wander about the center, but it was as far as we could go. This was it, our Mt. Fuji experience.

Like school kids on a field trip, we encircled a diorama of the mountain. Miniature light bulbs indicated rest stations along the winding trail that snaked to the top. I pushed a button. A light bulb flashed on. Asia stood across from me and smiled. She hit a button and another light bulb flashed on. Then more buttons were pressed and the model lit up like a Christmas tree.

What to do next? Ascending a back staircase, we entered a snack shop on the mezzanine. Normally one could buy tea, cold drinks, and snacks and eat everything at tables in the middle of the room, but the tables had chairs stacked on them. An attendant who was sweeping the floor looked at us with unmasked surprise.

Next to the staircase were two coin-operated machines that dispensed Mt. Fuji souvenir key chains. Asia and Robyn fluttered over to the machines like moths to a flame. The machines were bilingual. By turning a wheel, one could imprint a message in Standard English letters or Japanese *katakana* phonetic letters, onto a gold-colored disc.

Robyn conferred with her mother, inserted some coins into the machine, turned the wheel, and spelled out "Inaba Ladies Tour." She did that four more times and gave one to her grandmother and each of her aunts. I took mine out of its plastic case. It was bright and shiny with the date and picture of Mt. Fuji etched onto it. Our gold metals. Inaba Ladies brave Typhoon Opal!

I was beginning to get a little droopy and bought a package of *gyoza* or steamed dumplings and dried fruit to pump up my sugar level—the cost: ten-dollars and seventy-nine cents.

Across from the coffee shop next to the entrance of a darkened theater, a wall-sized picture of the snow-covered mountaintop was painted on a sheet of hard plastic and illuminated by lights. We stood in front of the picture and handed Ken our cameras. Same picture, ten times. Satisfied that we had exhausted all activities in the center, we headed back to our van. The fierce winds drove the rain sideways and turned our umbrellas inside out. Good thing we only had to go a few feet or we would have been blown inside out as well.

Ken asked our driver to circle around Lake Yamaguchi. The driver did not want to. Who could blame him—after all, we were in the middle of a typhoon. But Ken told him that we were from America, etc., etc., and the poor guy's Japanese compliance would not let him refuse.

We drove on a narrow winding two-lane road and I could barely see the lake through the storm. Brightly painted swan boats, like the ones at the Public Garden in Boston (only bigger) were moored to a dock. The boats bobbed furiously up and down on the choppy waters. I tried to get a picture of them, but everything was a blur.

The mountainside was verdant and interspersed with sprays of lavender wisteria. We drove into a little village and even through the downpour, I could see that it was quaint. One and two-story wooden buildings, the storefronts of shops and restaurants, were set into the hillside. One of the restaurants had Dutch doors with the top half open. The *noren*—shop curtain strung from the transom—turned and twisted like storm flags on a sailboat. I would have liked to have gotten out and explored, but the wind gusts exploded and whipped up the drenching rain. Water rushed in rivulets down the narrow streets. Our driver was sweating bullets trying to keep the van on the road.

Lunch at a French restaurant was included in our tour. We arrived early without appetites, ate wilted green salads, and then drove to Hakone, our last stop for the day. It was still storming outside, and our driver who was anxious to get back to Tokyo, took off the minute we stepped out of the van.

Hakone is the location of natural hot springs. It was featured in the *Travel Section* of the *New York Times* earlier in the year, so I knew that it was famous for tourists coming to take a good soak. Hot springs to me were always *onsen*; locations of hot mineral baths where old people like *Ji-chan* and *Ba-chan*, Grandpa and Grandma Inaba, went to rejuvenate.

> *Ji-chan and Ba-chan spent a week at a hot springs in California. Mom drove to pick them up, and I went with her. I was about thirteen at the time. I think one or two of my younger brothers, maybe Harley and/or Don who would have been nine and six respectively, was with us. Ji-chan and Ba-chan stayed in a little cabin. A big outdoor swimming pool was located on the grounds, and Mom said we kids could go swimming. I was surprised when I jumped in and found that the water was warm, almost hot.*

Hakone is fifty-six miles southwest of Tokyo. We stayed at the Palace Hotel, a contemporary building set into the side of a hill. There were just a few guests besides us. The hurricane was certain to have kept many people home. The hotel was small compared to our hotel in Tokyo, and our party took up practically an entire wing. Diane and I were unpacking and I opened a closet door and found a "sanitized" paper banner across hotel slippers. I called Diane over to show her, excited that I had made the discovery. She was usually the first to spot these things: the inspector, entering a room, sniffing the air, pulling back the bed sheets, and opening the dresser drawers.

I went down to the lobby to browse through the gift store. In a dining room across from the gift shop, Ken Suzuki was eating a bowl of noodles. He informed me that he could not get a train home and planned to take the first one back to Tokyo in the morning. He did not look happy or unhappy, just resigned.

The *ofuro* or bath, was at the end of the wing in which our rooms were located. Ten of us traipsed to the bath in cotton kimonos, *yukata*, provided by the hotel. We walked into a well-lit changing room. Everything was white. White wall, white counters, white towels. White jumped up, bounced off the lights, and boomeranged from mirrors. The whole effect was dazzling.

In contrast, the room where the bath was located was dim and the mood serene. Hot water trickled into a tear-shaped sunken tub. Steam vapors rose and fogged a glass wall. Showerheads were mounted on a tiled wall, and beneath them sat small plastic stools and buckets. Unlike other foreign tourists, we knew the drill. We washed and rinsed ourselves under the showers, then settled in the tub submerging our bodies up to our necks.

Outside, the wind howled and splattered rain against the glass. Muted green blotches, the shapes of bushes and branches, bobbed and waved from an enclosed garden. Inside, we reposed in the steamy bath. It could have been a tranquil Zen moment, but we were a lively and raucous bunch, our voices and laughter echoing off the water and walls.

> *Ten goosey ladies,*
> *In soothing ofuro. HONK!*
> *Storm rages outside.*

Dinner was in a sit-on-the-floor Japanese style private dining room. We were tired, ate very little, and went to bed amidst thunder and lightning.

Saturday, 21ˢᵗ of June 1997
Hakone to Nagoya to Toba: Ise Grand Shrine/ Meoto Iwa

The morning broke brilliant as only the day-after-the-storm-morning can. Mt. Fuji, hidden in yesterday's hurricane, appeared in perfect, dazzling clarity.

We had breakfast vouchers and ate in the dining room. I had an American breakfast of ham, eggs and rolls, and of course coffee. Besides our party, only one other couple was in the restaurant. I thought perhaps that they were travelers from Mexico because they conversed with each other in Spanish but spoke English to the waitress. We greeted each other. They were very pleasant, and left for the train station before we did.

After breakfast Diane, Lynne and I went for a walk on the terraced grounds of the hotel. We wandered into a greenhouse and found shelves full of potted African violets. A groundskeeper tending the plants seemed amused by our presence. We were speaking in English, and I do not know if he was amused because we were *gaijin*, foreigners with Japanese faces; or because he thought we had traveled thousands of miles to tour his workspace.

We walked to the front entrance of the hotel and found our entire party in the parking lot. From where we stood, we had a perfect view of Mt. Fuji. Out came the cameras. Taking turns, we took pictures using all combinations of people and poses possible against the backdrop of the elegant mountain. Who needed an illuminated plastic picture when we had the real thing?

Asia was on the mend and had more energy. A day of mainly riding in the van and going to bed early was probably the best medicine for her; but Cindy had a throat tickle and presented a new worry.

We rode the hotel van down the hill to the Atami Train Station. After a short wait, the Hikari #107 Bullet Train all sleek and white pulled into the station. Out came the cameras. Click went the shutters. I could see the captions underneath the photos in the albums: "This is us on the Bullet Train."

Bullet trains run nationally, and we rode south and east through rolling hills planted with tea. We rode through Shizoka, past modern houses with an air of prosperity about them. It was an hour-and-twenty-minute train ride. I dozed a lot. Standing on my head in time was catching up with me.

We changed trains at the Nagoya Station, and waiting to meet us on the platform was an old friend of my father, Mr. Ito. His wife and daughter Mariko were also with him. They were not going anywhere, just meeting us amidst all of the commuters and travelers.

After we moved to New York City, GT and I hosted scores of friends and relatives who came to visit, wanting a taste of the Big Apple. Sometimes we met them at airports or bus terminals, but mostly we gave them directions to our apartment or their hotels. We never met anyone on the platform of Pennsylvania Station as they were making a fifteen-minute connection to another train. We would have been jostled or cursed or pushed onto the tracks.

Mr. Ito looked like a typical Japanese grandfather with his gray hair and glasses. He had been a childhood friend of my father, both of them growing up in Walnut Grove, California. I conversed with him in English, and he explained that his family had moved to Japan after the war. He had married a Japanese woman and had three daughters. He and Dad had stayed in touch with each other, and when his youngest daughter Mariko was a teenager, she spent a summer in California with my family.

My sisters and sisters-in-law all knew Mariko, bubbled around her and popped questions. She was reserved and had the half-mast eyes of most Japanese ladies.

Our platform visit with the Ito's ended by the arrival of our new tour guide, Makiko Kumasawa who carried with her ten box lunches. She was a student-type, grown-up woman who wore glasses, was of medium height with a slight boxy build. We said our good-bys to the Ito's and boarded an express train to Uji-Yamada.

Our private van was waiting at our destination to motor us to the site of the Ise Grand Shrine. On the trip over, Makiko-san ran down an abbreviated history of the Ise or O–Ise Shrine. According to Japanese mythology, key artifacts belonging to the principal deities of Japan are stored on the grounds of O–Ise.

Makiko-san had the habit of repeating everything she said: "There is the sacred sword…sacred sword," she said. "The sacred scroll…sacred scroll. And sacred horse…sacred horse." It was like having an echo throughout our tour. She told us that certain structures were taken apart and rebuilt every twenty years so that each generation could participate in keeping the legend alive. I tried to think of a Western equivalent. Perhaps, if the Greeks stored certain artifacts attributed to Apollo in the Temple at Delphi and rebuilt it every twenty years, it would be like the O-Ise Shrine.

We spent the morning walking the grounds. It was more rural and spread out than the Meiji grounds in Tokyo. Tame carp or *kói* swam up to us as we sat on rocks that lined their ponds. The pool of *kói* became another photo op. "Asia, you and Cindy sit there. Then Steph and Robyn. Then Lynne and Diane. Judy, look up and smile." I snapped a half-dozen pictures of everyone leaning over blurry fish figures, blotches of orange with patches of black and white.

Off to our next stop. We rode along a winding two-lane road next to the coastline on the Pacific Ocean side of the island of Honshu. To our right, the ocean broke into a rocky sea cliff. It was like riding down a shorter version of Highway 1, which runs along the California coast.

The sun was beginning to lower on the horizon. Pearl beds hugged the shoreline. Makiko-san disclosed that this area was known for its "Hen-pecked…hen-pecked husbands," because the women pearl divers made the money for the household while the men were left to tend to the children and household duties.

The road took us to an inlet cove where the waters were calmer and the sea broke in small patches onto the rocky shore. Our van pulled up next to a tented area that sheltered tables and stalls. It looked like an open marketplace where vendors sold pearl products, but I could not really tell because by the time we de-vanned they were closing for business. It would have been nice if we had arrived earlier and been able to shop, but the upside of having gotten to this destination late in the afternoon was that we had the sunset pretty much to ourselves. It was a tough trade-off.

A gravel footpath curved along the shoreline, and below us perfectly symmetrical square logs were fitted together in a crisscross pattern; wooden breakers that jutted into the sea. Stationed in alcoves next to the water along the path were stone good-luck frog statues. I made Lynne stand next to one and took a picture.

> **Calm sea, Ise Bay.**
> **Lynne kissed the frog prince. And "Poof!**
> **He turned into Bob.**

In the distance was the famed Meoto Iwa, the wedded rocks: two boulders rising out of the sea bound together with a rope. Makiko-san explained that every New Year's Eve villagers climb the sides of the rocks and change the rope.

> *The lavender sunset casts a magic spell, weaving together the sky and sea into a blue-black silky backdrop. Segue into midnight. New Year's Eve. Hundreds of lanterns bob in small boats on the choppy waters. Voices float and echo as villagers climb the rocks, carrying the rope to bind them together for another year.*

Mom related that when she was growing up and heard stories about Meoto Iwa, she envisioned two huge rocky peaks like the glacier-carved granite domes in Yosemite rising out of the ocean. When she saw them for the first time, she was sorely disappointed. Still, in this early sunset against the backdrop of the sea, they were quite beautiful.

We left the sunset and headed to the Toba Hotel Internationale where we would be spending the night. At the top of a steep hill on a narrow twisting road, we pulled into a circular driveway.

The hotel was a split-level structure with the entrance, lobby, and dining room on one level, and guest rooms on another. Staircases and a corridor connected the two wings. A large photograph of Queen Elizabeth II (circa 1970s) was prominently displayed among the photographs of dignitaries who had been received at the hotel.

We had our own welcoming committee. Waiting for us in the lobby were Mr. Ito's daughter Mrs. Kato, and his teenage granddaughter Ikumi. American home stays for young people are quite popular in Japan, and Mrs. Kato had driven to the hotel to ask Mom if she would play host-family for Ikumi later that summer. Her request was previously made and accepted; but when the Katos learned we would be staying in Toba, they felt it necessary to formalize the request in person. Like the Itos' visit with us on the train platform earlier, face-to-face greetings, however fleeting, were considered common courtesy for the Japanese.

We had dinner reservations in a restaurant on a boat permanently moored to a dock below the hotel. To get to the restaurant we descended a steep hill on a plainly defined but narrow footpath under the thick boughs of pine trees.

A sign that advertised "Seafood Barbecue" sat on the dock outside the boat. Our dinner was pre-paid as part of our tour and was again, as had been the case throughout our trip, too much food for women with light appetites. I finished what I could, took a mint from a bowl next to the cash register, and stepped out onto the dock.

The air was crisp and clear. A near-full moon hung in the sky over the sea. Asia, Cindy, Steph, and Robyn came out of the restaurant; Lynne, Mom, and Sharon followed them; then Judy and Diane exited last. We wound our weary ways up the hill and back to the hotel.

> *Moonlight sprinkles path.*
> *Ten ladies on summer tour*
> *Climb pine-scented hill.*

Sunday, 22nd of June 1997
Toba to Osaka to Kyoto: Takaraduka

I awoke needing to exercise. We had done a lot of walking, but I had not jogged since San Francisco. I pulled on my jogging clothes, eager to get out. It was another overcast day, but the air was clean and scented with pine. Over to one side of the hotel, a footpath circled around a gazebo and connected to the main road. It was the only road to the hotel. No chance of getting lost.

Jogging downhill was easy and I followed the curves in the road, setting an easy pace. I rounded a bend, and discovered a woman walking up the hill toward me. This is what I saw: green babushka, brown sweater, blue skirt, sensible shoes—a hotel worker. This is what she saw: oversized white T-shirt, gray-running shorts, rumpled gym socks, sneakers—an aberration. We nodded politely as we passed each other.

Branches thick with pine needles arched in layers above me. Through the trees, smoke arose from the chimney of a cozy little house set in from the road. Below me appeared the roof and platform of a train station, and to its right the sea cut jigsaw into the coastline. An unpaved path veered off the main road and took a sharp downward turn. At that point, I turned back and ran up the hill to the hotel. All together, the trip down and back was no more than three-quarters of a mile. Despite the short distance, I was refreshed from the exercise.

I got to our room, undressed and showered. The bathroom was an inside one with no windows. There was a sink, toilet, and bathtub with shower curtain. It all looked clean, but with no window, all of the moisture from my shower lingered in the room. Heaven only knew how much mildew was lurking behind the curtain. I thought I should warn my roommate, but she was still asleep.

Buffet breakfast was served in a dining room that overlooked the water. An "American Style" breakfast with ham, scrambled eggs, and rolls served on one long table; and a "Japanese Style" breakfast on another. Since miso soup was the only recognizable dish on the Japanese table, I helped myself from the American side.

Coffee was served in demitasse-cups. One gulp, it was gone. I asked the waitress to bring me more. Halfway through my meal I asked for another refill. The waitress looked at me like, "Really? Another cup?" And I looked at her like, "What? You never heard of the bottomless pot?" (She obviously had not because years after our trip, I learned that we had run up a fifty-dollar coffee tab.)

We went back to our rooms to get our bags, and I asked Diane about the bathroom. "It isn't bad," she said. "They must rinse it out with Clorox every day. I can smell it."

We rode the hotel van down the same road on which I had earlier jogged to the train station that I had earlier seen. Counters displaying pearl products were set up inside the station. Mikimoto, the internationally known pearl jewelry manufacturer had a booth. A good selection, but the presentation was not nearly as elegant as in their New York store on Fifth Avenue. We looked but did not buy. Well, maybe, Lynne bought.

We boarded a local train, the Kintetsu Line to Osaka. We were traveling southwest, inland through hilly terrain.

> *When I was little, our family would often take summer vacations to visit Aunt Hisae, Mom's sister, in San Francisco. Dad woke us up before dawn. That was his style. We'd load ourselves into the car—all six kids and Mom, Dad and Ba-chan. Just about the time we got to Modesto and turned west, the sun would begin to rise, its rays illuminating the foothills outside Alameda County. Someone, maybe Mom, would begin to sing, "I-ma wa ya-má ná-ka; I-ma wa ha-ma…" And we would all join in.*

As our train wove through the mountains, and threaded in and out of tunnels, past villages where the rooftops of temples appeared in the distance, each verse of the childhood song came to life.

About an hour into the trip, a prisoner wearing an orange jump suit, his wrists and ankles shackled in chains, was escorted up the aisle by two prison guards. Diane, always looking to record a "Japan moment," elbowed me. Bowing her head ever so slightly, she muttered the Japanese equivalent of "Excuse me." *"Sumimasen,"* she said and boxed her hands in front of her eyes like a camera. She turned toward the prisoner, who by that time had been led up the aisle so that only his back was visible to us. *"Shashin-o,"* or "May I please take your picture?" I laughed aloud, but I suspect Diane's dark sense of humor would be lost on most Japanese.

Taeko Murata, our new guide, was waiting for us on the train platform in Osaka. We followed her up a deep, wide bank of escalators into the station. It was busy. Sunday was a big shopping day. We stored our luggage in lockers and went across the street to a big indoor shopping mall, then took an elevator to a food court on the top floor. Taeko-san explained that we would be staying at the hotel that was located at the other end of the mall when we came back through Osaka in a couple of days.

Our tour included food vouchers for lunch, and we scouted the mall and zeroed-in on a noodle shop. I order rice and *nattō,* fermented soybeans that are stringy and slimy in texture. When we were little my brothers, sisters, and I used to call it *kusái mamé* or stinky beans because of its slightly rotting odor. Definitely a dish for someone with an acquired Japanese palate.

"*Nattō?*" Taeko-san queried. "I thought because you were from America, you didn't know *nattō.*" If she only knew. *Nattō* was a staple when we were growing up.

We needed to go to the women's room before we headed out. As in most parts of the world, there was a line at the door. As we got closer to our turns, we found there were plenty of stalls but only one Western style toilet. All of the other toilets were squats. Yuck! Our party elected to wait for the western toilet and nine of us stood in one line so we could sit instead of squat.

Back at the train station, Taeko-san helped us get tickets to our next stop: Takaraduka. "Takaraduka" is the name of an all-female theater company. It is also the name of the place, Takaraduka Park, where the company performs. The concept was a little like the Rockettes meet Great Adventure.

Taeko escorted us to the entrance of the park. Inside the gates stood souvenir stands and a gift shop that sold Takaraduka memorabilia, but most of the area was occupied by a large modern theater. Asia made a beeline for the gift shop. She scanned through the merchandise with lighting energy, and purchased a package of baseball-type cards with pictures of Takaraduka actresses. Every thing was written in Japanese. She is gutsier than I am. I once bought a Japanese brand potato-slicer thinking it was a bottle opener and have since avoided purchasing anything with a description that I could not read.

We filed into the theater and had excellent views of the stage from plush red velvet seats in the first tier mezzanine. A good number of people were already seated, and it was still early, usually an indication of a full house. The audience was primarily women. I guessed that they were mostly housewives on their Sunday outing. At home, we would call them "Takaraduka groupies."

The show was presented in two acts. The first act was a historical dramatization about Japan in the Meiji Era as it moved towards Westernization. The hero of the script, the last Japanese samurai, was played by an actress dressed in warrior garb who spoke in a low male voice. The actresses who played roles of male government officials were costumed in Western-style military jackets and trousers. The only woman's part, that of the samurai's consort, was played by an actress wearing a kimono. One of the stage sets for the drama was a Victorian-style study furnished with a table and chairs. In the scene, performers dressed like midshipmen from Annapolis conferred around the table.

English subtitles were not provided, but I got the gist. The characters in military uniforms were calling for the unification and modernization of Japan. All of the fiefdoms had to be disbanded, and the lords who ruled them had to agree to give them up. Everyone was asked to make sacrifices. The samurai's woman did not want him to go on being a warrior. In the end, she died, and he nobly sacrificed his lifestyle for the good of Japan. He laid down his sword and the curtains closed. Women in the audience were openly weeping.

The second act of the program was more light-hearted. The company performed a medley of songs from various Broadway musicals and movies from the 1950s. The women who sang as men had deep baritone voices. The finale was the Takaraduka rendition of "Begin the Beguine." I did not recognize the words, but I knew the melody and recognized the Ginger Rogers and Fred Astaire clones who sang and danced against a Manhattan skyline backdrop. Ginger in flowing white chiffon was perched on the top of a winding staircase, and Fred in classic tux danced toward her. They both sang in Japanese. She floated down, and they twirled on the stage together and the entire company joined them. The song ended, and the curtain came down to great applause.

We filed out of the auditorium along with the other women who were heading out to prepare for their workweek. At the station, we collected our bags from the lockers and boarded the train to Kyoto. It was late when we arrived, and we rolled in cabs to the Hotel Fujita Kyoto, where yet another relative was waiting. This uncle was Mom's second stepsister's eldest daughter's husband. We bowed greetings and distributed *omiyage,* and then we went to our rooms and crashed out for the night.

Monday, 23rd of June 1997
Kyoto: Three Temples/ One Castle/ One Shrine/ and a Geisha House

A cemetery lay beneath our hotel room window. It was a small plot of land with headstones marking ashes. The Japanese custom is cremation, so I knew no bodies were rotting just outside our window; nevertheless, the close proximity of the graveyard to the hotel was my first clue. As cities go, *Kyoto is not Metropolis, Superman.*

I had no time to jog. We were scheduled for a full day of touring, and then dinner with Katsuyuki and Junko Iwata, who had met us in Tokyo. I calculated that I had just enough time to find take-out coffee and light breakfast.

Kyoto is a hilly city full of trees. I followed a street that sloped down to a river, and crossed over it on a narrow bridge just wide enough for pedestrian walkways and two lanes of traffic. At regular intervals, several bridges crisscrossed the river, lacing two sides of the city together. Lured by the sight of ever-present vending machines, I entered an area of small businesses. Buildings made of wood no more than two stories high lined the sides of the street. Pictures of *donburi* and *udon* dishes were taped to the windows of some of the storefronts, but the shops were not open. The street was quiet. No pedestrian or vehicle traffic.

I was not as lucky as I had been in Tokyo scoring *teuku autou*, but then Kyoto is not Tokyo. Kyoto is old. Much of the classical architecture is still intact. There were no tall buildings marking commercial centers, and the streets were not laid out in urban grids. My Manhattan navigational skills had failed me, and I headed back to the hotel empty-handed.

Diane was up and ready to go. We both needed our morning caffeine fix and went down to the lobby. Tucked into a corner was an area with small tables and chairs. I sat down. Diane stood across from me. "Leslee," she said, "We're in a bar. I saw it set up last night." At that point, I did not care. I wanted coffee! I told her to sit and stay. I flagged down a woman clad in a hotel uniform, and ordered two cups of coffee. It was served in tiny teacups, cost seven-dollars a cup, and barely made a dent in my morning craving.

The rest of our group was gathered in the lobby waiting for our private van. Lynne, who had witnessed the coffee transaction, just "tssked" at us. "Seven bucks for a cup of coffee? You guys are crazy," she scolded.

Asia and Cindy were bright-eyed and bushy-tailed. Cindy had gotten over her sore throat, and had more energy. I asked Asia what they had been up to. "Watching Japanese television," she said. Then she and Cindy sang "*Cha-ka, cha-ka, cha…Cha-ka, cha-ka, cha,*" and made rotating motions with their hands and arms, like kids do when they sing, "The wheels on the bus go round and round." "What's that?" I asked. "Some television commercial," they answered.

The "Inaba Family Japan Tour" van with Taeko-san already aboard pulled up, and we were off to our first stop: the Nijo Castle. We entered the grounds through a large wooden gate. A garden opened up to the right of us, and the entrance to the castle at our left.

The sky was overcast and set a mood of gloom that surrounded the castle and enhanced its history. According to pamphlets, it had been the center of the powerful Tokugawa Dynasty and undoubtedly the site of hundreds of conspiracies, co-conspiracies, and counter-conspiracies.

Everything about the castle was pure and authentic. The dark stained wooden pillars, hand-carved overhead beams, floor-to-ceiling sliding panels, and wooden platforms that outlined the entire building were all vintage Seventeenth Century Japan.

The floors of the outer platform surrounding the castle were constructed to squeak whenever anyone walked on them. The shogun who built the castle thought it was a clever way to detect a spy who might be sneaking about. Our footsteps made audible sounds, more of a "thud, thud" than a "squeak, squeak." Maybe it was because we were heavy-footed Americans and not light-footed Japanese spies.

Two small outer chambers stood at the entrance to the castle. The first was where a visitor presented his identification, and the second was where he waited while his identification was being verified. Behind the outer chambers were three separate receiving chambers, each one placed slightly off-center and behind the other. The innermost chamber was the shogun's living quarters. Where one was received was determined by one's relative loyalty to the shogun.

Sliding screens that separated the chambers were works of art. Taeko-san pointed out a gold screen with tigers and explained that since tigers are not native to Japan, the artist used cats as models. Sure enough, the tigers looked like round fluffy cats with ferocious faces.

Pine trees, bamboos, flowers, and birds were painted on screens and panels. Peacocks, cranes, and butterflies were carved into the open wooden beams above the doorways. Each of the chambers had a dropped panel ceiling made of square hand-painted wood tiles. The motif for one room was flowers, and each tile was painted with a different kind of blossom.

In the innermost chamber—the shogun's residence—mannequins portrayed the life of Seventeenth Century aristocracy. A shogun mannequin sat on his mat, and two ladies-in-waiting were kneeling in the foreground. Another lady-in-waiting stood holding a tray with a teapot and cup, destined to forever serve the shogun his tea.

We exited the castle into a quiet garden landscaped with pine trees and three ponds. It was classically Japanese, and its design replicated in American parks from Brooklyn to San Francisco. We bought postcards and picked up more castle handouts.

The Imperial Family took over the castle when Japan became a unified country, and in modern times, it became the property of the City of Kyoto. It had been preserved, but not particularly well maintained. Most of the panels needed restorations. An interactive visitor center where I could have learned its history before I ventured in would have been helpful. Still, it is a beautiful old building.

Our next stop was the Kinkakuji Temple or the Golden Pavilion, a square pagoda-style building that is three stories high, painted metallic gold, and crowned by a golden phoenix perched on top of a torii style roof. The Pavilion sat at the end of a still pond, its image reflected in the water.

"The Japanese writer, Mishima, you know Mishima Yukio?" Taeko-san asked. We nodded. "He wrote a famous book about the Golden Pavilion. He committed *seppuku*. You know *seppuku*?" I nodded. The proper Japanese term for hara-kiri or as my American friends said, "harry-karry." Mishima was a relatively young man when he died. Perhaps like the phoenix or the structure itself destroyed by fire and rebuilt several times, he thought to go out in a blaze of glory to be reborn again.

Entering the grounds into a clearing, we had a perfect view of the Pavilion, an ideal spot for a photo op. This was where I learned how pushy the Japanese could be. A group of people entered the park about the same time that we did, and then another group of men came in after us. We let the group who came in with us take their photos at the coveted spot, but as we moved in to take our turn, the group of men charged in front of us. One of them even had the nerve to wave us away with his hand.

Being ladies, we waited until they were through, but I was fuming inside. We took our places quickly so as not to let that happen again. The men, however, would not clear the camera area, so we had to squeeze together and even then we were sure to have a stray arm or the back of someone's head in our photos. I wanted to wave a magic wand and turn our polite group into working women from the Bronx on a subway platform at rush hour. There would have been enough elbow power to chuck the entire male chauvinist lot into the pond.

The Pavilion itself was closed to the public, so we toured the grounds on a pebbled footpath in a garden dense with summer trees and shrubbery. Foliage was so thick that we could not see what lay around the next bend. We were eager to explore and bounded forward like unruly school children on a field trip, leaving Taeko behind. We were delighted to discover a small pond with stepping-stones, and hopped over to the other side. The path continued for a while, then forked. I glanced up and caught sight of a sign pointing *THIS WAY*, but we had been going *THAT WAY,* all along. We turned around and retraced our steps.

> *Charge! Goosey ladies*
> *Hopping through green-leafed garden.*
> *One way, the wrong way.*

In contrast, the grounds of our next stop the Heian Shrine resembled a football field: flat, barren, open, two structures on each end. According to Taeko-san, it was a replica of the Empress' grounds and primarily used for weddings.

There is a certain point in any tourist's experience when things begin to meld. If you are touring the English countryside, all of the castles cascade into each other; if you are in Greece, all of the ruins seem to run together. It was at the Heian Shrine that I got shrined-out. It had no distinctive features and I felt like, "Seen one Shinto shrine, seen them all."

Our venue for lunch was "the famous Kyoto Handicraft Center." I had been looking forward to this stop, hoping for a chance to buy some nice ceramics and silk. The Handicraft Center was a square seven-story-high concrete building, its appearance incongruous with the rest of the low traditional-style buildings in Kyoto. That should have been my first clue. We walked into five floors of tourist schlock, commonplace merchandise that could be found in J-Towns and or Chinatowns from San Francisco to New York City. It was a letdown, in more ways than one. Running around all morning with minimal food intake caught up to me. I had my first major sugar drop in the Kyoto Handicraft Center.

A feeling of clamminess seeped through my body. I felt faint and lightheaded. Sharon was standing next to me. "I've got to eat something, now!" I said. A sign advertised buffet lunch on the sixth floor, and we rode an elevator to a cafeteria: metal tables and hard plastic chairs, a small steam table, a stack of dishes, and orange plastic trays. The staff was putting out the food: overcooked pasta, mushy rice, bits of chicken and carrots. The most unappetizing mess I had ever seen. The cost, 1400 yen or the equivalent of about twelve dollars.

Lynne came up the elevator looking for us. "Taeko-san knows a restaurant nearby, and we're going to lunch outside." she said. I wanted to go in the worst way, but I was afraid I would pass out. I told Sharon to go with them, but she was locked into the role of the care-giving big sister and insisted on staying with me. We took our trays and spooned out a little rice, and chicken with carrots—*more carrots that chicken*. Sharon insisted on paying the bill, a total of about twenty-four dollars for us both.

The elevator door opened and a multi-racial tour group of about a dozen people stepped out. Most of the people were Caucasian, along with one couple of African descent. The tour guide was a short, stocky Asian woman wearing a Hawaiian print shirt. They were clearly Americans. The tour guide said something in Japanese to the cashier, and then addressed the group in English. "Your vouchers are good for lunch. You can use your vouchers here." Sharon looked at me. "They shouldn't bring tourists to a place like this," she said. "They're going to think all of Japan has terrible food."

We ate quickly and left. My body had stabilized, but my mind was still reeling from my twelve-dollar meal of rice and bits of chicken and carrots. We headed outside to look for the rest of our group who had disappeared into the winding streets of Kyoto. Deciding it would be futile to try to find them, we settled on exploring the neighborhood.

The morning haze had dissipated leaving the sky a blue wash. Dark chocolate colored buildings with peaked roofs and upturned smiling cornices lined the streets. Every fifty feet or so, red and gold flashed from birdhouse-like structures tucked into alcoves between the buildings.

"Look at that," I said. "I know, they're all over," Sharon replied. "What is it?" I asked. "I think it's a family shrine or something." "Go stand next to one so that I can take a picture." I ordered, changing the tables on her. "You want to take a picture of that?" Sharon balked. "Just go over there." I commanded. And she did, and I took a picture of Sharon next to someone's *kamidana*, a family shrine.

We wandered down the street and looked into the window of one of the shops. Inside was a low counter and two chairs, and shelves full of boxes and packets of teas. An open bin of tea leaves stood to the side of the counter. A woman was tending the store, and Sharon went into the shop. I meandered to the end of the street, and then went back to join her.

Sharon was sitting at the counter sipping tea and nodding her head. "Try some," she said. The woman put a cup in front of me. I sipped the tea. It was mellow with a light hint of grass. Sharon asked the woman what kind of tea we were drinking. She did this in Japanese. The woman answered her, also in Japanese. I nodded, pretending that if I wanted to, I could talk to them too.

So there we were, me and my big sister sipping tea in a no-nonsense Kyoto tea parlor, as if it was something we did every Monday afternoon. Sharon was comfortable in this element, closer to the language and customs of Japan than her siblings. I simply followed in her wake, flying beneath the radar. I ended up buying two boxes of tea, and Sharon bought more.

We walked out of the shop, and Lynne came up to us. "Umm, umm," she said licking her lips with the brat trait that comes with being the youngest sister. "Taeko took us to a noodle shop. Best lunch we ever had."

We joined up with everyone else and headed out to our next stop, the Kiyomizu Temple. The van deposited us at the bottom of a large hill thick with trees. The temple was built into the side of the hill and we made our pilgrimage up a dirt footpath. Beneath a canopy of leaves, open-air kiosks displayed colorful dishes, toys, and trinkets, and lent a medieval festival atmosphere to our walk. I purchased a small clay bell shaped and painted like a tiger. It looked like a fluffy cat trying to look mean, and since I knew the story about "no tigers in Japan," the whole effect was precious.

A large wooden balcony jutted out of the hillside and overlooked the city. The foundations for the temple and balcony were built and reinforced with large square logs cut to fit into each other. No nails were used in their construction.

Wooden beams crisscrossed up the hill. Dodging the sheltering limbs of trees, a few rays of sun tumbled off wood posts, and lit onto the trail. A rocky wall enfolded the side of the hill. In the background, the sound of water cascading and splashing into a pool. Green velvet moss coated the rocks, wood, and trees, layering all in a film of tranquility. Corralled behind a stick fence, a stone lantern and *jizō* statues adorned with red bandanas.

When Asia was about three years old, GT read bed-night stories to her from a book of Japanese fairy tales. One of her favorites was about a monk who wanted to cross a river but was too lazy to try. He fell asleep on the riverbank, and along came a band of monkeys. Thinking that the monk was a jizō, a statue representing the guardian and protector of all children and travelers, the monkeys hoisted him onto their shoulders. The monk awoke as he was being carried into the river, and realizing it was an easy way to get across, he decided to keep his eyes closed and pretended he was a jizō. Then the monkeys began to sing: "We don't care if our feet get wet. We don't care of our tummies get wet. We don't care if our tails get wet. Just keep the jizō dry!" It was such a silly song, that the monk began to laugh. Realizing that the monk was not a jizō, the monkeys promptly dumped him into the river. Asia and GT would march around our apartment singing, "We don't care if our butts get wet. Just keep the jizō dry!"

I told Cindy to stand in front of the *jizō* so I could take a picture. She did, striking a "Here-I-am-with-the-*jizō*," pose. She obviously was not tuned into the serenity mood.

At the foot of a stone staircase, Mom elected to stay below while the rest of us trudged up to a rocky platform. Above us, three streams converged and flowed over an overhang, creating a waterfall. Behind us a series of religious altars were tucked into the crevice of the rocky cliff.

The water from the falls was reputed to have great healing powers. Long-handled tin cups rested along a railing at the edge of the ledge. Fellow pilgrims crowded around the railing, and as spaces opened up, we extended our cups into the waterfall and sipped the liquid that splashed into them. We came down from the temple feeling self-righteous. We made the effort to drink from the stream, and were sure to be rewarded.

At the bottom of the staircase, Mom met us carrying a bottle of water. "What's that?" I asked. "Oh, it's water from the stream. I got it over there." And she pointed to a shelter where attendants were dispensing bottled water. "And we had to climb all the way up there to get ours?!" I exclaimed. Mom just laughed.

We posed for group pictures on a wide platform that is supposed to overlook the city of Kyoto. I am sure it does, but it was the middle of summer, and all that was visible was a sea of green treetops. Both Cindy and Asia were in high spirits, and made the peace sign with their fingers, then went into being *cha-ka, cha-ka* girls.

By the time we left the grounds of the Kiyomizu Temple, it was late afternoon. We had one more stop for the day, the Ryoanji Temple that featured the famous Zen rock garden.

During the New Age craze in the U.S., all-things-Zen increased in popularity and one could purchase a miniature tabletop rock garden: a wooden box, gray and white gravel, blue-black pebbles, and a tiny wooden rake. We were about to see the real thing.

The Ryoanji Temple is a low simple structure, designed along the same classical lines as the Ninjo Castle that we visited earlier that day. But all similarities ended at the exterior of the two buildings. Whereas the interior of the Ninjo Castle was decorative and ornate, the interior of the temple was bare in its simplicity.

I walked along the narrow ledge lining the temple and sat down in front of the world-renowned Zen rock garden. A sea of gray and white pebble swirled around fifteen moss-covered boulders. A dark clay wall provided background for contrast and defined the garden.

Lynne came over and sat down next to me. We looked at the boulders. The puzzle posed by the garden is, regardless of the angle from which it was viewed, one could not see all fifteen boulders at the same time. We counted eleven, then tried from another angle, and counted thirteen. It had been a long day. I was low on energy and too tired to meditate.

> It was close to noon when we pulled up at the top of a mesa overlooking the Painted Desert. Dad had rented a van, and it was to be our last family vacation together, ten days through the southwest: Nevada, Arizona, New Mexico, and Colorado—to the site of Amache Relocation Center where our family had been interned during the war, and where Sharon and I were born. We had been on the road five days. I stepped out of the van and Lynne came up behind me. It was a hundred degrees and still rising. Across from us multi-layered sandstone buttes rose out of the badlands. The sunlight bleached all the colors into varying hues of gray. No other colors, just gray. "This is it?" Lynne asked, "the Painted Desert? I'm not impressed!"

We looked at the rock garden. Perhaps its enchantment had been washed out by overexposure and commercialism. For me, there was no magic, just rocks.

In the back of the temple under maple trees, a small stream spilled into a rock-lined pond. Water filled one end of a hollow bamboo log. Upon reaching a certain level, the log tilted, spilled its contents into the pond, and bounced off the rocks with a soft "pong-pong." Judy stood on the ledge next to the pond. In the whole of Japan, she declared that this was her favorite spot. And despite our fast-paced day, she looked refreshed.

We returned to the hotel with enough time for a short rest and change of clothes. Katsuyuki and Junko Iwata were taking us out to dinner. When they called for us in the hotel lobby, Junko was chatty and informed us that she had something special planned.

Following our hosts, we headed down towards the river on a narrow curving pedestrian pathway. Stained wood-plank fences lined both sides of the road. Peering over the tops of the gates, I caught glimpses of potted plants and little yards leading to sliding paper doors.

On the road ahead of us were two women dressed in beautiful silk kimono, their obi flowing down their backs. One of them turned her head slightly exposing the white pancake make-up of a geisha. "They're *maiko*," Sharon said. "They are not really geisha, but geisha-in-training." Lynne and Judy were ahead of us, and stopped to take pictures. Then all of our cameras came out, and we took turns taking the same picture a half-dozen times. Junko tried to hurry us along by telling us that the surprise she had planned was to take us to a geisha house after dinner.

The street on which we traveled led to the river, and the water level was summertime-low. We descended a stairway beneath a narrow bridge and walked along a worn footpath in the riverbed. A woman wearing a long blue dress walked ahead of us, her footsteps kicking up puffs of dust that twirled and danced with the hem of her skirt. A little girl in red shorts and white T-shirt ran squealing and laughing next to her.

Wooden decks jutted out over the levee above us, and Junko identified them as expensive restaurants mainly frequented by businessmen.

We walked along the river from one bridge to another (about the distance of ten city blocks), mounted a steep path, and ended up on a street. Junko and Katsuyuki led us into one of those expensive restaurants that we had seen from the riverbed. We were conspicuous because of the number of females in our party. The maitre d' led us through the main dining room and out onto a deck that overlooked the river. Four low tables had been reserved for us, and we sat on the tatami-matted floor.

On the shore below us, a young man reclined across the top of a flat boulder. Hands pillowed the back of his head, eyes closed as he soaked in the slanting rays of the setting sun. A young woman sat next to him and hugged her skirt around her knees. Her gaze was as much inward with her thoughts, as it was outward across the river. A boy toting a book bag gleefully romped along the riverbed kicking up stones.

> *Setting sun settles*
> *Everyday lives. Perched on deck,*
> *Touring ladies dine.*

Junko took out a video camera, turned it on, and scanned our group. We all waved to her, and Sharon said something in Japanese. Then Junko pulled out a little basket and revealed that we would have a private drawing. We each took turns pulling a number from the basket and were awarded a prize. I got incense and an incense holder.

We were served more food that we could possibly eat, managed what we could, and then headed off to our next adventure—a geisha house.

The house was set back from the road and we passed through a gate up the front walk to a paper-screened door. A teenage girl in a T-shirt and blue jeans slid aside the door, took our wraps, and put away our shoes. Out from the back of the house, an older woman clad in a dark kimono emerged, greeting Katsuyuki. He had obviously made arrangements with her, and we followed her into a back room and sat on tatami mats around low tables. She asked Katsuyuki what we wanted to drink. We had just eaten and were not big drinkers. Our order: two beers, two teas, and eight cokes.

Two *maiko* entered the room carrying trays full of drinks. One *maiko* wore a dark blue kimono with white and light blue butterflies, and the other was costumed in an aqua kimono with pink flowers.

> *Aqua background and pink flowers painted on folding fans. Obon Odori. The dance festival for lifting souls into heaven. August night. Fresno's desert air. Bottles of strawberry soda cooling in tubs of ice. My sisters and I dressed in kimonos. Obi tied tight, wrinkling our bellies. Japanese music played over a loudspeaker. We followed dancers in a circle, three blocks long. Arms arc, bodies twirl, silk kimono sleeves flutter like flags under paper lanterns.*

The *maiko* sat on their knees behind us. Then another *maiko* came into the room. She wore a navy blue kimono with bright red and white flowers. She had a little kitten face and a "mew, mew" voice. She took command. Her ability to speak English was better than the others, which was not too difficult since they spoke no English at all. They referred to her as *onesan,* or big sister.

The *onesan* asked Cindy, Asia, Steph, and Robyn their ages. Mom answered her in Japanese that they were between the ages of twenty-two and eighteen. We asked her how old she and the other *maiko* were. She replied they were eighteen and nineteen. The *onesan* explained that they started training at the age of sixteen. They all began their service like the girl in blue jeans who met us at the door, and gradually got to do more geisha duties. They came from different villages outside of Kyoto City and lived in the geisha house. On New Year's Day, they were allowed to go home and visit their families. It was their only day off.

Besides the white pancake make-up on their faces and necks, they had darkened eyebrows and bright red lipstick on their lower lips. Our girls asked them how long it took them to apply their make-up, and the *onesan* replied she spent twenty-to-thirty minutes. She explained that she set her hair with lacquer once a week and slept a on high round pillow. Asia asked, "Did you always want to be a geisha?" "Yes, this is what I want to do," she responded.

And she was very good at it. The *onesan* kept the ball rolling. I am sure that ours was one of the most difficult parties she would ever host. We were eleven women and one man. Most of the eleven women did not speak Japanese. The youngest of our group was one year her junior, and the other young women were only slightly older than she. Most of us were old enough to be her mother. One of us was old enough to be her grandmother. And the other woman was the man's wife.

For the next hour, the *maiko* entertained us. They danced. They played games with the girls. Our girls, in turn, showed them their *Tamagochi,* their virtual computer pets, and conversed in what little Japanese they knew.

Asia had taken one semester of Japanese her first year at college, and when she said, "*Ni-hon-go wa, mu-zu-ka-shi, nei,*" I knew Brown University was doing a good job. "Japanese is a very complicated language, isn't it?" was one of the two phrases she had retained. Mom was impressed.

Junko kept the video camera rolling the entire time. At the end of the evening, we bade goodbye to the charming *maiko,* and Junko and Katsuyuki walked us back to our hotel. As a final surprise, Junko disclosed she planned to send each of us a videotape of the evening. Junko is amazing. She had organized and managed an evening we would never get on any tour. I hoped someday to be able to reciprocate her kindness and generosity.

Tuesday, 24th of June 1997
Kyoto to Nara to Osaka: Nara Park/ Todaiji Temple/ Kasuga Shrine/ Osaka Castle

It promised to be another hot, humid day. Before we left the States, Judy gave the over-forty contingent in our group neckerchiefs with cooling gel. *Soak the scarf overnight in a sink full of cold water. Tie it around your neck. Guaranteed to keep you cool in hot, humid weather!* And this was the day we needed them. As if by plan, we all showed up at our motor coach with cool-aid neckerchiefs tied around our necks.

Diane sat in the window seat beside me, and I fell asleep the minute the driver turned the key in the ignition. Only once did I open my eyes to glimpse a blurred green countryside whiz past me.

I awoke as tires crunched gravel and the van pulled into the parking lot of Nara Park. I wished I had been able to stay awake for the drive because Diane reported that we had ridden through beautiful countryside. "It was the Japan I'd always imagined!" she exclaimed.

Nara Park is famous for its herds of tame deer, and—looking like extras from *Bambi*—they approached us as soon as we got out of the van. Some were small, but a good number were big with large antlers. The park sold animal feed in the form of crackers, and Taeko bought a package to share. We watched a man hold a cracker over the head of a doe. The animal bowed its head three times, and was given the cracker as a reward.

Some of the deer were not well-behaved and snatched crackers out of people's hands. A young antlered buck approached Taeko-san. She got nervous, threw the crackers at him, and ran away. I noticed that the deer did that mainly to women. I decided that I was not going to let them push me around, so when one came up to me and did not bow, I bonked him on his head until he did.

Sharon said, "Don't do that. They'll get mad and come after you." I was too stupid to care. Asia was not afraid of them either. But when one of them did not bow for her crackers, she just spoke to it quietly, and it politely bowed three times. The deer are an odd mixture of timidity and aggression, much like a larger version of the squirrels in New York City parks.

The park grounds were level and sparsely treed with well-defined pedestrian paths crossing the middle and along the outer parameters. At one end of the park, a massive two story wooden gateway marked the entrance to the Todaiji Temple. Lynne and Judy stood beneath the gate and I pulled out my camera, but had to keep backing up in order to get the all of the gate into the frame. When I finally got the entire structure into the picture, the individual features of pedestrians at its base were indistinguishable from one another.

Beyond the entrance, a huge bronze Buddha sat on a large open outdoor platform. Taeko explained that this area was where Japanese Buddhism was first established. Very impressive, but at that point, I was getting Buddha-ed out.

Since we missed the boat ride at Mt. Fuji, the travel agency was throwing in a group picture in Nara Park. The Japanese are honest. In New York, if you miss anything because of weather conditions, you were pretty much out of luck. A professional photographer lined us up, shooed over four deer to pose with us, and snapped our picture. With our "cool-aid" neckerchiefs, we looked like a Girl Scout troop.

The Kasuga Shrine was our next venue. This shrine was composed of thousands of moss-covered stone lanterns on a hillside under a forest of shading trees. Our footsteps crunched dry leaves into the gravel trail. Sunlight filtered through the branches and the hazy day gave the hillside a kind of "Twilight Zone" affect. Taeko-san explained that there were close to two thousand lanterns, and lighting ceremonies conducted twice a year.

Our last stop for the day was the Osaka Castle Museum. We approached it by walking over a pedestrian moat. The Castle loomed before us, built in tiers wide at the base and narrow at the top. Three triangular rafters with pointed peaks climbed upward and atop the castle perched on the highest peak, a gold fish arched its tail into the sky.

Inside on the seventh floor behind viewing boxes holographic figures depicted the life of Hideyoshi Toyotomi. Press a button, look into a box, and images of *ojisan* and *obasan* bowing in front of a modest house on a modest farm came to life. Move to the next screen, and view the next chapter in the life of one of Japan's most powerful rulers.

One other notable exhibit in the castle museum was "The Summer War of Osaka." Miniature samurai armies faced each other on a battlefield behind a glass display case. I had seen tiny British and American soldiers set up this way at the Bunker Hill Monument in Charleston. And my brothers had played with small plastic army men with rifles and machine guns. But this was the first time I encountered samurai action figures with swords and crossbows.

The modernity of the museum turned out to be a preview of the city of Osaka. From the top of the observation deck, a panorama of the city with its tall buildings, highways, and major league baseball park expanded before us.

We arrived at the Miyako Hotel and learned that Kumiko's mother and sister Noriko had been waiting in the lobby. Mom invited them up to her room so that we would have a chance to meet the family of our soon-to-be sister-in-law.

Mrs. Inui is a small, cheerful woman. We felt at home with her right away. She gave us each a copy of the book "Japan at a Glance," for which Kumiko was a major contributor. Noriko is Kumiko's older sister and I felt she could fit right into our group. She was personable and greeted each of us individually. I would love to have her come to the U.S. and run the streets with us, but Noriko was afraid of flying.

I said, "Noriko, Doctor *ni i-ki-ma-shi-te, ku-su-ri o mo-ra-i-ma-shi-te, hi-ko-oki ni no-ri-ma-shi-te*" (my elementary Japanese got me as far as saying: "Noriko, doctor, go to, medicine, get, airplane, get on,"). Then I acted like I was going to sleep, and opened my eyes and said, *"So-shi-te ka-ra, o-ki-ru to-ki wa, A-me-ri-ka!"* Viola! Awake in America! I think she understood what I was saying to her, although I may have been a little vague about using tranquilizers to get through the trip.

The Inui's took their leave early to allow us to rest. The next day we were on our own—no tour guide, no castles or temples or shrines. I took the subway map of Osaka from the front desk to study and then promptly fell asleep.

Wednesday, 25th of June 1997
Osaka: On our own

This was the day our party split off in separate groups with separate agendas. Mom, Sharon, and Judy were scheduled to go to Kobe to meet with business associates. Diane, Lynne, Steph, Robyn, and I were on our own. Cindy was somewhat travel-weary, and she and Asia elected to tootle around the immediate area.

Lynne was looking for a BB gun for one of her sons, and acquired the name of a hobby shop. We were going to get directions when we met Judy, who was with her friend Michie Marutani.

When Harley and Judy were living in Japan, they resided in the same apartment complex as Michie and her family. Since their children were about the same ages, Judy and Michie struck up a friendship. Before our trip commenced, Judy wrote Michie and informed her that she would be in Osaka, and Michie came to meet her.

"Michie was a real life saver," Judy explained as she made her introductions. "She helped me get my kids to doctors and buy medicines when they got sick." Michie was about five-feet tall and thin in stature. Age-wise she was in her mid-forties. She had a nice smile but very sad eyes. We bowed our greetings and went on our way.

We approached the reception desk, and Lynne showed a young clerk a slip of paper. "Can you tell us how to get here?" I asked. The clerk looked at the paper, then looked at us. She clearly had, "You want to go *there*?" written all over her face. But she took a subway map from the pile on the desk and circled a stop.

I looked at the map. Six subway lines crisscross through Osaka. The Miyako Hotel where we were staying was on the Tanimachi Line at the Tanimachi 9 stop. We were two stops away from Namba, which appeared to be a major station. Okay, so far so good. Going the opposite direction, we were four stops away from the Abeno station and the shop was two stoplights from the station. How hard could getting there be? But just in case we got lost, I took some business cards from the hotel so we could flag a cab to get back.

We were off! We sailed though revolving doors and came to a dead stop. "Where are you going?" Lynne asked. "The clerk said the train station was that way, not this way." "I think it's this way," I retorted. Diane just rolled her eyes. I looked up and Michie was walking towards us. In perfect English, she informed us that she had forgotten to leave something with Judy. We told her that Judy had already left for Kobe. She asked us where we were going. I showed her the map.

She gave us the same look that the clerk at the hotel had given us, and then said, "Do you want to go there? I will take you." We did not want to bother her, but she told us that she had taken the day off from work and did not mind. Michie became our lifesaver. I knew how Judy must have felt those years ago when she was living in Japan.

We walked to the subway station, which was across the street from the hotel in a direction neither Lynne nor I had been headed. A row of machines lined one wall. Tickets were dispensed automatically and priced according to one's destination. It would have taken us months to figure out, but we just did as Michie instructed and were through the turnstiles lickity-split.

The subway trains are smaller and somewhat cleaner than they are in New York City. We rode on an elevated track close to buildings. Through windows, I saw rolled futons, low tables, tatami mats. Between buildings, small concrete yards with potted plants. The scene was entirely Japanese Urban.

We stopped at an intersection where three blocks converged at one point. Across the street was a bank with an outdoor ATM, and among the banking logos displayed was *NYCE,* the network to which our bank in New York is linked. It was the first time I had seen *NYCE* since landing in Japan, and I suddenly felt connected to home.

Michie led us down a street that ran parallel to and under the train tracks. It was a major thoroughfare, and on either side were two and three-story buildings. We were in a nondescript commercial area. Nothing around us would have been of interest to tourists, but we were on a mission.

We walked the requisite two stoplights, and two doors from the corner Michie pointed out a street-level shop with boxes of model airplanes and automobiles in the window. Inside the shop, Lynne asked questions with Michie translating.

It turned out, no, they did not have the kind of BB gun that Lynne was looking for, but they did have another kind of air gun, which Lynne immediately bought. The salesman explained the gun could not be fired without an air canister, and Lynne bought that too. Seeing the gun and canister in Lynne's hands suddenly set off warning bells in my head. We had been so focused on finding the shop that it did not occur to me until that moment that the merchandise was certain to be on the contraband list at the airport.

"How are you going to get that through airport security?!" I demanded. Lynne glared at me with a *drop-dead* look. She bought the gun, and that was that! I backed off, leaving it her problem to solve.

Our first successful excursion on our own—well almost on our own—and we were hungry. We tumbled into the street and discovered a cozy sandwich and noodle shop clean enough to meet with Diane's approval.

Stephanie and Robyn sat at one table, and Diane, Lynne, Michie, and I at another. Michie's command of English was impressive. She never had to grope for words, or run phrases through a language translator. I was curious, and over a crustless egg salad sandwich with Japanese mayonnaise and a cup of green tea, I learned more about her.

"Where did you learn to speak English?" I asked. She responded with ease and honesty, allowing me to visualize snap shots of her life, clear black and white stills.

Michie in her early twenties, her eyes sparkling, carefree and happy, living in India and working for a Japanese firm. English, the medium of communication allowing her access to local residents. Perused by handsome Indian men.

"I liked it there, but my visa expired and I had to come back."

Michie with a Japanese man on their wedding day. He is wearing a suit, she a dress. A look of resignation in her eyes, reconciled to the reality that it was time for her to settle.

"What does your husband do?" I asked. She wrapped her hands around her teacup as if it might warm her, and looked down at the table. "He is sick. I must work." She worked at a factory that made small tools. "The work is not hard, but the pay is low. I had a good job at the Holiday Inn. The pay was good, but the work was hard and sometimes I had to stay long hours. Then I got sick, and had to quit." "Do your children go to school?" "My son works at a gas station. My daughter is sick and stays home. She makes things." And Michie showed us a glass bead and macramé key chain. It was a charming trinket, and she smiled as she held it up.

We headed back to the train station and wandered though an open building with commercial booths. Packaged confectionaries, zori, plastic samurai swords, assorted sundry products—nothing caught our interest. Michie asked what we were looking for. "Just shopping," we replied. She told us she would take us to the Namba shopping district where she and her daughter liked to go on weekends.

Around the Namba Station, we finally found a serious shopping area: an arcade-style mall with covered walkways and big department stores, including

Tiffany. Across one of the walkways, a couple of Häagen Das signs were prominently posted on the walls. I made our party stand next to the sign so I could take a picture: "Häagen Das in Osaka."

We entered a major department store and rode up the escalators. Women who appeared to be in their late 40s greeted the customers at the top of each stairway. On one of the floors, the greeter was short and pudgy and had an obvious black dye job. She asked us where we were from. Michie replied that we were sansei from America. The woman said she had read about how Japanese Americans were locked up in camps during World War II. I said, "I was born in a camp." Michie translated. The woman was shocked, then cried and hugged me and said, "*Yoku nata ne.*" She was so relieved that it all turned out well, and that I grew up happy and healthy. Lynne found the whole scene hilarious and started to laugh. I was both touched and embarrassed. I hugged the woman back, and we went on our way.

Our hotel was close to the shopping mall and we easily walked back. We thanked Michie for all her help and gave her some *omiyage*. She smiled her melancholy smile and thanked us in return.

Asia was in the lobby. "What did you do today?" I asked her. "I went shopping." "Where?" "There's a shopping area a couple of blocks away with a bunch of stores," she replied. She had easily stumbled on what took us all day to find.

Judy got back from Kobe, and came to our room. "How did you get around?" she asked. "No problem. We went all over on the subway train." "Did you get lost?" "No, your friend Michie took us. She was great." Judy was visibly relieved.

I was curious about Japanese working class women my age. Do they all stay at home? What if they can't? What do they do for work? The Japan Times, an English language newspaper provided by the hotel, listed a number of clerical positions in the employment wanted section. Along with the usual clerical skills, a proficiency in Japanese and English defined qualifications. Michie with her command of the languages should have been a shoo-in. However, each of the ads ended with the same unabashed statement, "Must be between twenty to thirty years of age." Or sometimes more sharply stated, "Over thirty need not apply."

Obviously the Japanese have never heard of age discrimination. When we were touring Tokyo, I remembered Ken Suzuki telling me that ethnic Chinese and Koreans living in Japan, including those native-born, could only hope to reach a certain level of employment. It appears that discrimination in employment is the accepted norm. The Japanese have no inherent political tradition that assumes that all men, and women, are created equal. Not having that as part of their societal mores, they neither expect nor demand it. For all of the efficiency associated with Japan, there is still a vast waste of talent.

We had been invited to have dinner with Mom's stepsister Aunt Shizuko and a number of cousins, none of whom I had ever met. *Ji-chan* Hamaoka, my mother's father had been a widower with two daughters prior to having married my grandmother. Aunt Shizuko was the youngest of the two.

Ji-chan's story reads like so many Japanese men who immigrated to America in the early 1900's.

> *Two brothers sail to America to seek their fortunes. One takes his family with him. The other, a widower with two daughters, leaves them in the care of family members, fully intending to return to Japan a rich man. The conditions in America are harsh. The work is backbreaking, and he is lonely. A young woman from his village comes to America. By a stroke of luck, she is single and available. They marry and have three daughters. His brother finds life in American too difficult, and moves his family back to Japan. But the man stays and works hard, still believing that someday he too will return to Japan and his entire family will be reunited.*

> *Then Pearl Harbor is bombed. War is declared. All communications between the U.S. and Japan are severed. In the U.S., the man is detained by the F.B.I., labeled an 'Enemy Combatant', and held in a prisoner of war camp in New Mexico. His wife and daughters are interned in a relocation center somewhere in the Southwest. He worries incessantly. Loses his health. By the time his family members locate him, he is a broken man. He is sent to the camp where his family is living, and when the government closes the camp, he and his wife move with their eldest daughter and her family to Denver.*

> *Atomic bombs are dropped on Hiroshima, then Nagasaki. The war ends. The man and his family move back to California. His American daughters seek out their stepsisters in post-war Japan. One is found still living with the relatives with whom she had been entrusted, but the whereabouts of the other is lost. It is reported that all official family ties with that sister ended when she disobeyed family wishes and moved away to become a nurse during the war.*

> *In the early 1950's the man dies. Twenty years later, his wife passes away. Another decade goes by, and then a cousin from Japan visits the U.S. From her comes news of the second stepsister. She had married and lived in Nara. Letters are exchanged, and visits occur. The family is at last reunited.*

We had dinner with that once lost sister, and the guest list read like a reunion of the "McCoy Clan." There was cousin Akiko and second cousin Harumi;

cousin Noriko and her husband cousin Shoji; and second cousin Kumi, and her two little boys, third cousins Suguro and Kaname. When Kumi was younger, she spent a summer in California with Lynne and her family. Kumi had since married and her sons typically pulled on their mother with a hundred demands during dinner. Harumi, our other second cousin, was going to university. She was the sophisticate in the family and appropriately dressed for a fancy dinner. I felt a little too casual, bordering on sloppy, next to her.

Both Kumi and Harumi sat at our table, and making conversation, Lynne in broken Japanese asked Harumi if she went to lots of parties and played around at school. Harumi laughed, and responded that she did her share. Then Kumi piped up and volunteered that Harumi was always playing, partying, and drinking. To which Harumi sharply retorted, (and I translate literally) "Ms. Kumi certainly seems to know a lot about my business!" Then everyone was quiet. The silence was a little awkward, but it was fun hearing a cat scrap in Japanese.

Aunt Shizuko was a frail eighty-one year old woman. After dinner she called both Asia and me over to her. She took our hands, and started to cry. She disclosed that she had hoped to see her entire family before she died, but when she visited Mom in California we were living in New York. Our dinner together represented a fulfillment of her wish and she was happy. Her family patted her on her back and looked a little embarrassed, like they wished she would not carry on so. I held her hand. For the second time that day, I had the humbling experience of being the object of undeserved affection.

Lost Aunt, found nieces.
Full Circle in Osaka,
Summer's setting sun.

Thursday, 26th of June 1997
Osaka to Hiroshima: Iwakuni/ Miyajima Island

5:45 a.m.: Two short rings. "Brinnng…brinnng." I am in a hotel room. I am in Japan. It is the phone. "Just calling to make sure everyone is up." Judy's voice was cheerful-tinted-with stress. We had been warned. We must catch the bullet train at eight-o-four. No guides to help us. The train waits for no one.

6:30 a.m.: Diane and I stepped out of the elevator into the lobby. A neat row of pink pom-pommed black bags lined-up along a windowed wall. "Here they are!" Lynne exclaimed. "Who's missing?" "Cyn and Asia," Steph replied. "We're right here." Asia reported. An elevator door closed behind her.

Our party huddled together in the center of the lobby. Particles of anxiety orbited around us. "What's going on?" I asked Sharon. "Those business associates from Kobe insisted they drive us to the train station. Yesterday when they were bringing us back, they got lost and we kept riding around and around."

What to do, what to do!? Wait for our ride and risk missing the train? Or be extremely rude and leave without them? Judy made a decision. "Let's phone them now and tell them not to come. Maybe they haven't left yet." She and Mom hurried toward the public phones.

6:40 a.m.: Judy darted over to confer with the desk clerk and Mom rejoined the group. "No answer," Mom reported. "They must have left Kobe already. I told them that we had to be at the station by seven-thirty. I told them it was, *mō*, all right, but they insisted!" Judy rushed over to us and announced, "It takes fifteen minutes to get to the station by cab." "Even with cabs, we'll need more than one. We'll need three or four." Mom fretted. "If they don't come by seven we'll call for cabs." Judy declared.

6:47 a.m.: No van from Kobe. Ten pair of feet shifted nervously in place.

6:50 a.m.: "We're calling for cabs." Judy proclaimed. And she and Mom scurried over to the reception desk.

6:53 a.m.: Judy and Mom hovered over the desk, intensely planning our get-away. Then Judy shouted something to Diane. Diane repeated it to Sharon. "Get your suitcases and go downstairs." Sharon ordered. We grabbed our bags and lined up at the foot of the down escalator. Eight bodies with eight bags glided smoothly to the lower lobby.

7:01 a.m.: "They said to come back upstairs!" Lynne exclaimed. Eight bodies, eight bags lined up at the foot of the up escalator.

7:02 a.m.: "Stay downstairs!" Mom ordered as she and Judy rode down to meet us. We dropped our bags and waited behind glass doors.

7:13 a.m.: A black cab whizzed into the driveway. We surged out in mass.

7:14 and 7:15 a.m.: Two more cabs pulled up to the curb. We broke up into manageable clumps. Trunks popped open, bags piled in, passengers boarded. We sped up a ramp, made a hairpin turn, zipped past the main lobby where we had been assembled since six-thirty, and shot into the streets of Osaka.

Our cab driver was a chatty man who was not the least bit concerned that we might miss our train. He struck up a conversation with Mom. He asked her where we were from, and she told him that we were mostly sansei and yonsei from America. She gave him the "apology speech," that we are *dame*—no good—because we never learned to speak Japanese. He reported that young Japanese girls were more and more dating men of African descent, and said he thought they must be crazy. Mom did not respond. I wanted to say, "We'll have the race relations talk later. Just get us to the station!" But could not manage it in Japanese.

7:35 a.m.: Three back cabs pulled up at the curb to the train station. Everything that was done at seven-fifteen was done in reverse.

7:40 a.m.: We flew through the doors of a tidy, compact building with several sets of staircases and signs posted above them. Judy and Mom checked their itineraries and searched the signs. They checked again and scanned again, and finally pointed to a set of stairs at the back corner of the building.

7:46 a.m.: We ascended onto a platform. Judy and Mom took another look at the signs and verified that we were waiting in the right spot. We had eighteen minutes to spare.

We collectively exhaled! The girls plopped on benches. I wandered downstairs and bought some crustless Japanese sandwiches from nearby food stands. As I climbed back to the platform, Mom reprimanded me. "Again?" she said. "Leslee, don't buy us any more food. If you want some, just buy for yourself!"

I nodded, but I knew that I would not. I could not help it. Maybe it was because I am diabetic and do not want to be caught in a drop; or I am married to a chef and used to having food around; or I just can not resist getting something that is fresh and looks good. Probably all three. At any rate, we once again were fixed with food for our train ride.

A Bullet train pulled into the station. This time no one pulled out a camera. Bullet trains were becoming old hat. Or maybe we were just tired from all the adrenalin spent on the fifteen-minute cab ride that took over an hour. We boarded, I ate a sandwich, and fell asleep.

At our destination, we were ushered into another Inaba tour van by our new guide Hiroko Kashiwa. Hiroko wore glasses and her mannerisms were much like our other guides except for one subtle, almost undetectable difference. She was completely at ease with us. Nothing we said or did surprised her.

Hiroko's pediatrician husband had studied under a medical fellowship at the University of California in Los Angeles, and they had lived in Santa Monica. Her children had attended a university-run cooperative childcare center, and she sparkled when she talked about her American experiences. "Japanese women love living in America. This is not so true for Japanese men," she disclosed.

We disembarked on the bank of the Nishiki River. Across the river, a tree-filled hill rose steeply, and at the top was the Iwakuni castle—white, majestic, impenetrable. A wooden footbridge arched over the river in five separate arcs as though it was playing leapfrog over itself to the other shore. Full of gender-conscious tidbits, Hiroko informed us that before Japan's modernization, only samurai were allowed on the bridge. Everyone else had to traverse the river by boat. And for a long time after the common man was allowed on the bridge, women were not.

Crossing over the bridge itself was an adventure. Our footsteps bounced off wooden planks and echoed off the water. Five or six samurai running across the bridge in wooden-soled *geta* would sound like an entire army.

Hiroko, Diane, and I reached the peak of the highest arch. I glanced over my shoulder and caught Asia, Cyn, and Step skipping playfully over the top of the arc behind us as though they were on the road to Oz.

We landed at the entrance to the Iwakuni Village; a testosterone-tinged *Samurai Land*, like a cowboy town in the Wild West with dirt footpaths and wooden fences. Spartan buildings that had housed warriors in service to the lord were converted into a museum. Behind a glass display case lurked white snakes with ruby eyes! (At least, it was advertised that they had ruby eyes; when we saw them they were curled up with their heads tucked into thick white-rope bodies.)

The hill behind the village was so steep one could only reach the castle by footpaths or a sky tram. The hill and the river provided natural protective barriers. If those were not enough, the nest of samurai living in the village must have served as a deterrent to any invading army.

We climbed back over the five-arched bridge and drove to a restaurant for *okonomi-yaki* lunch. As soon as we were seated in tatami-style booths—faux floors with cubicles cut away under low tables so that our legs could dangle—a waitress came over and started up the burners on hot plates atop the tables.

Okonomi-yaki was one of Judy's favorite dishes. It was one of those things that was like something else, but not quite. Like an omelet, but a little thicker; like a pancake but not as thick. You had to eat it to get it. An egg batter cooked on the grill was its base, and one added whatever ingredient was on the menu. I ordered *natō*. Hiroko did not blink an eye. If *she* had been with us when we were going the wrong way on a one-way path, *she* would have turned us around.

After lunch, full and satisfied, we waited at the Miyajima-guchi station to catch the ferry over to Miyajima Island. The forest area around the ferry building was home to deer in the region; they freely wandered in and out of the building, begging or demanding food from waiting passengers. One buck went right up to Diane and stuck his nose into her face. She was startled; he was not. He must be a buck from New York City. I think I have seen him work the subways.

A water jitney with capacity for about twenty passengers ferried us over to Miyajima Island. It was about a ten-minute boat ride, just enough time to be revitalized by the sea air.

Hiroko-san led us around the island into an alcove to the Itsukushima shrine. Another Shinto shrine. This one was built on a platform that extended into the sea. At the end of the landing, about two hundred yards into the water was a big bright orange *torii* gate.

We were the only people on the platform and it was a Kodak Moment. There was no need to squeeze together as we did at the Golden Pavilion. Hiroko-san snapped pictures of the group with ten different cameras. Then we took a picture of just the young girls, then one of grandma with the young girls, then one of grandma with her daughters, then Mom waived her hand and said, "*Mo-i*!" She had enough.

Many festivals occurred at this spot during the year. On New Year's Eve, young men light big torches at the mouth of the shrine, and the fire reflects off the water. I could understand its drama, yet for whatever reason this site did not hold any magic for me and I did not experience the kind of images that I had during our visit to the Meoto Iwa Wedded Rocks.

Our walk back to the ferry dock was more ambling than our walk to the shrine. This was often the case with sightseeing. When I showed guests around New York City I often rushed them from one spot to the next, and lost the discovery and exploration part of the adventure. As it was, there was plenty to discover and photograph besides the *torii* gate. Along the path, long white lanterns hung from the top of the entrance to the Komyoin Temple and deer grazed on its grounds. I told Asia to stand under the lanterns and took a photo.

We passed a compact little firehouse with fire trucks the size of mini-vans parked inside. Compared to American firehouses and trucks, they looked like miniature replicas. Accentuating the toy-like appearance was a cartoon figure with a punch-out head and fireman's body painted on a free-standing board. "Go over there and put your head through that hole," I directed Asia. She rolled her eyes and sighed, but did what I asked and I shot a picture of her face on the body of "Fumio the Fireman." Poor Asia. Since I was the mother, she could not just wave her hand and say, *"Mo-i!"*

The firehouse struck me as something uniquely Japanese. Japanese American firemen are so rare in the States. The firehouse confirmed for me that Japanese in particular, and Asians in general, are perfectly capable of putting out fires (although given the number of times we have heard of this temple and that castle burning down and having been rebuilt, I wondered if they could use some lessons from their Irish American counterparts).

The ferry bore us back to the station, and we journeyed in our van on a modern expressway to Hiroshima. It was not a long ride and within about an hour we were turning onto a ramp and crossing into the city. To our right stood the dome of the lone surviving building from the atomic blast nearly fifty-two years ago.

We rode along a river. The land markings around it were familiar. I recognized it as the same river that appeared in a grainy black and white documentary filmed hours after the bomb detonated. Dazed and burnt, throngs of people stumbled into the river to bathe their wounds. They could not see what the camera lens captured: flesh melting off bones.

> **River: Time's juncture.**
> **Ghosts from pi-ka do-n summer**
> **Creep into the day.**

Beyond the river, green treetops from the Peace Park reflected life and time past. We would be on our own for part of the next day, and I would go to the park to pay my respects.

Hiroshima is a very modern city. Our hotel was at one end of a shopping mall. We said good-by to Hiroko-san and gave her *omiyage*. For the first time, I realized that our stash of *omiyage* was running low, and we still had all of Kumamoto and our relatives to see. It is true what they say: you can not have too much *omiyage* when you visit Japan.

Our accommodations in the Rihga Royal were plush and roomy. Robyn and Stephanie shared a room overlooking a major league baseball park. The stadium lights were lit and the Hiroshima Toyo Carp were playing at home. It was like being in a luxury skybox. We had an unobstructed view of the field, and could follow play-by-play close ups on the television set in the room. Too bad the trip was all women. Our husbands, brothers, and nephews would have killed for this room.

The hotel brochure listed a swimming pool as one of its amenities and since I needed a good workout, decided to check it out. Stephanie was also interested in taking a swim and tagged along. We followed signs on the second floor to a glass-enclosed gym with an indoor Olympic-size swimming pool. A receptionist informed us that the guest user fee was ten-thousand-yen. Ten-thousand-yen was roughly ninety-dollars. Too steep for me! It was no wonder that Americans thought Japan was expensive. Seven-dollars for a small cup of coffee. Ninety bucks for a swim!

Friday, 27ᵗʰ of June 1997
Hiroshima to Hakata to Kumamoto

Mom, Sharon, Judy, and Robyn elected to stay at the hotel and the rest of us trudged off to the Peace Memorial Park. The day was hazy, slightly overcast, and humid.

It was the tail end of the morning rush hour, and the streets were crowded with pedestrians. When we first landed in Japan, the sea of Asian faces did not make any particular impression upon me. After all, since I live so close to New York's Chinatown, I could get a close-to-Japan experience (being surrounded by Asian faces speaking a language I do not understand) just by walking down Mott Street on any weekend. But on the streets of Hiroshima with hundreds of people ahead, behind, and all around me, I was struck by the incredible variety in the spectrum of Asian faces. Contrary to stereotypical thinking, we do not all look alike. At one point in our trip, Sharon said she thought the men in southern Japan were more handsome than the men in the north. I was just beginning to discern the difference.

The Peace Park is near the site of the hypocenter of the atomic blast. We crossed a pedestrian bridge and entered the park from its northernmost point where the Honkawa and Motoyasu Rivers meet. To the left and slightly behind us was the A-Bomb Dome, the spherical shell I saw from the roadway. It was the top of the only building in the area that remained standing after the atomic blast.

We took a footpath to the Hiroshima Peace Museum, a long, modern, two-story glass-enclosed building with two separate wings. Entering the Museum through the east wing, we crossed the threshold into a hushed quietness. There were only a few visitors, but even if there had been hundreds, the magnitude of the events that occurred over fifty years ago required reverence. In a matter of minutes, in what was described through words and pictures as "a white flash…searing heat…blasting whirlwinds," ***seventy-five-thousand*** people were instantly vaporized. One minute they were walking along, going to work, or riding their bikes to school; then in the next minute, they were gone.

One of the displays was simply a slab of concrete and piece of cloth. A striped pattern identical to the one woven into the cloth was imprinted into the concrete. A young man had been sitting next to a concrete wall when the bomb detonated. His body, along with part of his shirt, was forever etched as shadows into the concrete.

I had seen these images before. They did not shock me. As I wandered through the exhibits, I only felt that sense of odd detachment that museums produce. I was an onlooker viewing death and destruction from another time period, observing in these halls the result of ultimate technological devastation.

Near the exit of the building copies of letters addressed to every meeting and conference on nuclear disarmament since 1946 papered an entire wall. Written on behalf of the citizens and signed by every successive Mayor of Hiroshima, they echoed the call for a total ban of all nuclear weapons. The tone of the letters reflected a stubborn doggedness, like the character of "Watanabe-san" in Kurosawa's film, *Ikiru*.

We walked out of the museum into daylight. The sun broke through the clouds and promised unfiltered warmth and light. The park was quiet and lightly populated. We took a path that led to the Children's Peace Memorial, a metal structure built like a tower with a figure of a pre-adolescent child affixed to the top. One arm and one leg were extended as though he or she had just taken a great leap off the ground.

Garlands of colorful origami cranes lay at the base of the memorial. Children from Japan and all over the world had placed them there. I knew the story of *Sadako and the Thousand Cranes*—which told of a little girl dying of leukemia who folded cranes because she believed that a thousand folded cranes would bring world peace—but I did not know how the tradition of bringing cranes to this monument began. There must have been as many origami cranes as there were victims of Hiroshima and Nagasaki.

Crossing the footbridge that spanned the Motoyasu River, we headed out of the park. Modern Hiroshima invaded our world again. This must have been the way the people of Japan dealt with their devastation—by building the Peace Park where there are memorials to the victims, but no sense of victimhood. I did not detect any bitterness or outrage; or any echo of the post-war intellectual debate over, "Should the bomb have or have not been dropped." There was only the collective recognition of the event, the clear determination that it should not happen again, and the energy directed toward rebuilding the city.

We regrouped at the hotel and rode to the train station without incident. A Bullet Train, the Hikari #37 carried us to the Hakata Station where we transferred to an express train, the Ariake #15 to Kumamoto, the last stop on our tour.

I felt as though I was going home. Kumamato has always been a reference point in my life. *"Where is your family from?" "Kumamoto."* It is the birthplace of everyone I called *Ji-chan* and *Ba-chan*.

At four-thirty in the afternoon, the train pulled into the Kumamoto Station, a small station house with a ticket window opening onto the platform. Beside the platform parked in a rack was a bicycle. No lock or heavy chain, just the bicycle.

Hisakazu's father Mr. Iwata met us to walk us to our hotel. We did not have far to go since it was next to the station. After we checked in we took a streetcar designed like the old San Francisco cable cars to the mouth of a covered shopping mall. Mr. Iwata led us through the main walkway and down a side branch to Kenji's sushi shop. Kenji was the second in the line of three Iwata brothers. All were accomplished in the sport of judo, but Kenji unlike his brothers had a lean build. His face was thin and he had mischievous eyes. My hunch was he was the prankster in the family.

Kenji's shop was narrow and accommodated a sushi bar and counter. In the back was the kitchen and upstairs a room used for parties. We took up all the seats at the counter, and Mr. Iwata perched himself on a stool by the door.

The restaurant functioned with a three person staff. Kenji was the sushi chef, his wife Yuko was the waitress and bus boy, and his mother was the sous-chef and dishwasher. Kenji's three sons emerged from the back room. They were all tall and lanky. The eldest was about sixteen and the youngest about twelve and they appeared to be shyer than were their Tokyo cousins.

The phone rang. Kenji answered it and I heard him tell a customer that he had *okyaku-san* guests from *Amerika* and that the shop would be closed until six o'clock. While conversing with Mom and Sharon, Kenji rolled one piece of sushi after another. Perfectly formed mounds of rice topped with tuna, followed by yellow fish, followed by octopus, followed by eel—all incredibly fresh as though just taken from the sea—flowed from his hands onto our plates. Without missing a beat, Yuko and Mrs. Iwata picked up each separate plate as we finished. They moved so quickly I tired just watching them.

Kenji placed the *pièce de résistance* in front of us: a bright pink, paper-thin slice of lean meat on a small mound of rice. Mom sat on one side of me, and Diane and Stephanie on the other. Steph made eye contact with her mother and mouthed the words, "What is it?" Grandma caught the message, looked at her sternly, and mouthed back, "Just eat it."

We had been given notice. Horsemeat is a delicacy in Southern Japan. I willed away all images of *Black Beauty*, picked up the sushi, and ate. The meat was sweet and tasty. It was not the meat, but the thought of eating horse that stuck in my throat. I looked at my plate. There was another horsemeat sushi sitting on it. Diane looked at me from the corners of her eyes and smiled. I held my breath and ate hers as well.

Having been treated to an unforgettable meal, we cleared out of the restaurant so that Kenji could reopen his business. A little girl about nine-years of age buzzed around the front entrance to the shop. She chatted away with us in Japanese, and asked us where we were from and told us all about herself—like the fact that she went on a vacation to Singapore with her mother. Kenji explained that she was a friend's daughter who liked to hang out at the mall. They all seemed to think that it was a perfectly normal occurrence. A nine-year old girl hanging out on her own: an unlocked bicycle in a public place. Things are clearly different in Kumamoto than they are in Manhattan.

To exercise off some of the food we had eaten, we walked back to the hotel. Diane and I had a corner room on the third floor, and from a side window could look down onto the railroad station.

Close to midnight, I awakened with indigestion. I could try to blame it on the horsemeat, but it was a chronic condition that I had nursed since I landed in Japan. I got up and took an antacid. A streetlight showed brightly through the window, and below the last locomotive for the night slid into the station. I stood and watched as a handful of commuters spilled into the street and trudged their weary ways home. A young man mounted the bicycle and peddled away into the night. One light from the station house shined onto the platform. Otherwise the streets were quiet.

Saturday, 28th of June 1997
Kumamoto: Visit to the Inaba Homestead

The Iwatas had graciously volunteered to be our hosts for the next two days, and this was this our day to meet relatives. Our first venue: tea with Aunt Taeko Inaba on the family property where *Ba-chan* Inaba had been born. Three cars would be at our disposal. Kenji had taken the day off from his shop and would be driving his car. Hisakazu had come in from Tokyo and had enlisted the help of his sisters-in-law, Eiko and Takako and her husband Junichi.

We drove into *inaka,* the country on a two-lane winding road. Green hills cultivated with vineyards sloped around us. There were no road signs or signposts, or fences or structural designators. At a fork in the road, Kenji the lead driver pulled over and the other cars followed. Kenji stepped out of his car to confer with Junichi the driver of the second car. On a previous trip, Kenji had taken a wrong turn and he wanted to check his bearings. It would be so easy to get lost. Since the roads were not identified, how could there could be maps? Apparently, the right direction was chosen because shortly thereafter we were riding up a gravel driveway that curved slightly at the top of an incline and leveled off in front of a large modern two-story house. Three cars pulled over and parked next to each other in a clearing across from the house.

Aunt Taeko's two-story whitewashed house stood out against the lush trees and bushes that surrounded it. Stationed on both sides of the ridgeline on the roof were the customary gold fish. Along the side of the house were three long rectangle windows. We entered through a breezeway and removed our shoes in the vestibule or *génkan*. Inside was like a loft, a large open space with designated areas sectioned off by shoji screens and panels. A low table marked the living room, and we sat around it on tatami mats on the floor.

Aunt Taeko raised three daughters and perhaps that explained why I felt so comfortable with her. Though she spoke only Japanese, I understood almost everything she said. Over green tea and homemade *manju* or sweet-rice cakes, she explained that Grandmother Inaba was born in a house that stood at the top of the hill, and grew up in a house that was located at its bottom. A subtle but important distinction.

Ba-chan Inaba was the youngest of three children. Her father, my great-grandfather owned the land on which Aunt Taeko's house presently stands. As was the custom of the day, a childless Aunt and Uncle who lived down the hill adopted *Ba-chan* to prevent their family branch from dying out. So strong was the belief that one's name should live on, that when *Ji-chan* married *Ba-chan*, he took her surname Inaba since he had other siblings, and she was considered to be an only child.

The windows in Aunt Taeko's house were open, and the lingering laughter of little children mingled with the breeze and danced into the room. Over a hundred years ago, *Ba-chan* Inaba clad in a cotton *yukata* played in the vineyards below.

> **Moon face, twinkling eyes,**
> **Little girl romps, geta feet**
> **Swirling summer dust.**

Just as quickly as I had that image I understood *Ji-chan* Inaba, young and ambitious with too many dreams to stay a second family on the land.

I was grateful that Aunt Taeko had provided this opportunity for us. She had been to Sacramento and visited with Mom, and while they caught up on news about mutual friends and family members, I excused myself to go to the washroom. Sitting on the floor had stiffened my hips, and I limped when I took my first steps. When I got to the lavatory, I was surprised to find a squat toilet. With these living arrangements, I wondered how the Japanese could ever have hip replacement surgery without dislocating their hips. Moreover, I wondered how Japanese who have fused hips were able to function. Curious concerns for an American tourist in Japan.

Shortly after GT and I moved to New York City, I went to work for Dr. Philip D. Wilson, Jr., one of the pioneers of hip replacement surgery in America. I was part of the office staff, a secretary with clerical duties, and had at best a sketchy medical background when I started with him. Yet, here I was observing Japanese customs from an orthopedic perspective. Dr. Wilson is a remarkable teacher.

I got back to the sitting room to find the party breaking up. Our drivers taxied us into a village and our next stop was at a modest house on a narrow street. Sharon informed me that the *obasan* we were going to visit used to have a tobacco shop in front of her house, but she had retired and the shop was no longer there.

The *obasan* is a great aunt. She was short and bent over with a hump on the upper part of her spine, the telltale sign of scoliosis. Her condition did not appear to limit her motions and she moved quickly about. She led us inside and I was the last person in line and stopped to remove my shoes. Nine pair of shoes were disgracefully scattered over every inch of the *génkan*. Frankly, I was embarrassed. It looked like a day in the shoe store after an untidy customer had tried on every pair in the shop! I straightened them out, but just as I finished, the herd thundered out, collected their shoes, and piled back into the cars. I could only follow them, having missed whatever was the purpose of our visit while serving as shoe monitor.

We traveled a short distance to a restaurant and again disembarked. The number of people in our delegation constituted a natural party. Throw in second cousins, and a generous sprinkling of third cousins, and the only place big enough to accommodate us was the back room of the restaurant.

Seated next to my mother was her cousin Teiko Kiyama. I looked at them, then did a double take. Same jaw-line, same forehead, same build. I had never seen anyone, including Mom's sisters, who so resembled her.

> *In the Japanese American community where I grew up, no one looked like anyone else. Isei immigrated and stayed in ones and twos. Family for Mom and her nisei friends was Papa, Mama, brothers, and sisters. No uncles, aunties or cousins. Maybe there just were not enough of us to have a look-alike.*

Our relatives had ordered up Japanese *gochisō* a feast, and while we lunched a light rain began to fall. The Iwatas (seemingly not wanting to intrude on our party) took their own lunch and patiently waited outside.

After lunch we were invited for ice cream at Cousin Teiko's house. Adorning the walls were photographs of men proudly dressed in Imperial Army uniforms. It was very strange, seeing those photos. During World War II, these relatives were our enemy. Teiko informed us that she had never been to the U.S. Her husband was stern, a bit gruff, and said that he had no desire to go to the U.S. In him, I sensed some of the anger of the vanquished. But Teiko said that she would sometime like to make the trip. She was kind and gracious, and we thanked her and headed back to Kumamoto City.

The Iwatas had arranged for dinner in a restaurant that was in the basement of an antique shop. The food was artistically presented: splashes of orange and green on violet and purple plates trimmed in gold. Kenji's three sons and Takako's son joined us, and all of the girls and boys sat at a separate table so they might mingle. "How did it go?" I asked Asia later. "We all tried, but it was another painful dinner conversation," she replied.

Having been fed a huge lunch and too much dinner, I was up all night with indigestion.

Sunday, 29ᵗʰ of June 1997
Arita: Three Kilns/ A Ceramic Outlet Mall

We were joining the entire Iwata clan, making the head count twenty-two for the day, and Mr. Iwata had chartered a full-sized bus. Learning that we were interested in Japanese ceramics (although our interests were more consumer-oriented than that of art historians) Takako and Junichi had previously toured Arita, a city in the region of the Saga province famous for its kilns, and planned the outing.

I sat across the aisle from Yuko and asked her about the sushi shop. She replied they had closed for the day. I apologized for our being such nuisances, and she responded that she had been looking forward to having the day off. Then the bus driver started the engine, and she immediately fell asleep.

I tried my linguistic skills on Kenji. In my most thought-out Japanese, I said, "Your brothers moved to Tokyo and you decided to stay in Kumamoto." He replied, *"Okasan wa, sabishíi, kárā."* Or, "Because my mother would be lonely." He was very sincere, and I wanted to tell him that I thought he was a good son, but the only phrase that came to my mind was, *"Ii ko, ne!"* or "You're a good little child!" He was a bit startled when I said this and looked back at me. Then he realized that I was not kidding, and he burst out in laughter. Mom was right. I should have studied harder in Japanese school.

It was about a two-hour ride on a modern four-lane highway. The young people were in the seats behind us, and I heard a lot of attempts at conversation. It was mainly the big kids, that is, Yo-mei and Norio, and our four girls. Then someone broke out a deck of Uno cards, and there were many more attempts at explanation. I was not sure how much real playing went on, but there was a good amount of trying.

We took a travel break at a rest stop, designed like those on the interstate highways in the U.S.: a convenience store, lavatories, and parking lot. Feeling the beginning of a sugar drop, I headed for the snack shop and popped for a small seven-dollar bag of dried apricots.

On the sidewalk in the front of the store, a man was selling *square* seedless watermelons. For some reason, I never thought of watermelons as indigenous fruits to Japan; however, I could see that they were not only native, but had been hybridized. They were still very expensive, running anywhere from seven-hundred to one-thousand-yen for a small, cube-shaped melon.

After another hour we arrived at the Kakiemon Kiln where Akae porcelain were first produced. We piled out of the bus in front of a long whitewashed building with a thatched roof. Takako informed us that the building once housed a working kiln, and was currently used as a storehouse; the thatched roof was part of a recent renovation to give it historical authenticity.

Using the building as a backdrop, we lined up for group photographs. Fifteen cameras came out of their cases. Kenji was elected group photographer and clicked fifteen shutters of the same group with little variation.

Housed in a smaller adjacent building was a museum and gift shop. Behind glass counters were century-old ceramic wear. Akae porcelain was famous for its technique of polychrome overglazing. On a brilliantly white background, reds and blues and yellows and greens were overglazed to give the designs rich color and texture. The oldest piece dated back to the mid 1600's, about the time the Pilgrims were establishing themselves in Massachusetts.

Inevitably, it was Sharon who discovered the most affordable treasure. "Come see the *ben-jo!*" she exclaimed, pulling on my arm. I went out of the shop and into the women's room that was decorated from floor to ceiling in white ceramic tiles glazed with blue designs. The restroom took one's breath away—in a good way.

We returned to the bus and headed off for our second stop, the Gen-emon Kiln. It displayed what collectors know as "Old Imari." The kiln was closed to the public but across the road the gallery gift shop was open.

The pieces on display were designed in patterns I always identified as Imari. Intricate designs of red, blue and green accented in gold. However, I learned that the term Imari comes from the name of the port through which most of the ceramics passed on their way to the rest of the world.

On the other side of the planet delicate tea sets and plates sit in exhibition behind glass cases. London: The Victoria and Albert Museum. I wandered through the galleries, astonished that more than a hundred years ago, before cargo ship and airplanes, these fragile ceramic pieces were carted thousands of miles and found themselves in the homes of European royalty.

We stopped at a third kiln with yet another gift shop. Sharon reported that it was the Koransha gallery, but at that point all the galleries were beginning to glide into each other.

As our large party threaded its way through narrow aisles flanked with cases displaying exquisite Imari design pottery expensively priced, Grandma lost it for a moment. Handsome young Japanese men surrounded her four beautiful granddaughters, and she got excited by the possibilities. She pointed to one of the pricier items on display and told Stephanie, "I'll buy you one of these, if you marry a Japanese man!" As soon as she said it, she knew she had made a mistake, but it was *too late*! Four sets of ears perked up. "That's *blackmail!*" Steph said. "Do they have to be Japanese, or can they be Asian?" Asia asked. "How about Filipino?" Robyn added. Grandma got all flustered and had to take it back.

Our next venue: a paint-your-own-design studio and kiln. The building was long and narrow and designed like a potter's workplace. A worktable with jars of blue glaze and paintbrushes sat in the middle of the room. Along one wall, unglazed unfired cups and plates sat on shelves. And next to them, finished pieces were displayed for sale. A man stood behind a counter next to the front door to supervise and collect our money once we were done.

So there we stood, all twenty-two of us crammed together in a small work area. Hisakazu politely deferred to Sharon. "*Hai*, Etsuko-san." he said, referring to her by her Japanese name. He pointed towards the table. Sharon responded "No," and shook her head. Kenji said, "Norio?" Whereby his son vehemently refused. Then there were murmurs. All the adults urged the kids to decorate pottery, and all the kids held back. Again the adults urged on, again the kids resisted. The stand-off lasted over a minute, and I got antsier by the second.

Then it happened. The impatient New York demon that cannot tolerate polite hesitation reared its ugly head and took over my body and before anyone could make another refusal, I leapt onto a stool, grasped a teacup and brush and began to paint a design. Mom was mortified, but I could not take standing around like that for one second longer. Once the ice was broken, all the kids sat down and started to paint.

I finished decorating my teacup, got up, and observed. Robyn had obviously practiced this type of craft before and was making a pleasing piece. Asia was experimenting by applying lots of glaze to a plate. The big boys Yo-mei and Norio made designs specific to the date of our visit. The storekeeper recorded addresses where the pieces would be sent once they had been fired, and we all left in good spirits.

Our big shopping stop for the day was the Arita Porcelain Park, a mall of factory outlets about half a city block long. We attacked the shops like kids let loose in a strip mall full of toy stores. I did not have time to keep track of everyone else and headed right into the nearest shop. It was crammed with goods. Dishes and rice bowls flowed from the shelves onto the floor. Teacups and sake sets were stacked on top of cartons in the aisles. No way was I going to be able to look through everything, so I had to go with whatever caught my eye. I picked up a gray plate with four cats painted on it. I'd never seen anything quite like it and thought it would make a good *omiyage* for my cat-loving friends at home.

Asia came into the store in an active hunt mode, looked over all the goods and tried to find something for her friends. I walked out and saw Lynne and Steph crossing the center of the mall to explore shops on the opposite side. Diane and Cyn were more methodical in their search and went in and out of businesses that lined one side of the mall.

Having made dinner reservations, the Iwatas pulled us out of action before we really had a chance to make many purchases. The shopping gods would not be appeased that day. We rode back to Kumamoto City and since we had not been overfed, were famished when we reached the restaurant. The food was all very good, but I particularly enjoyed dessert. Served in a hollowed-out watermelon that had been decoratively carved on the outside, it consisted of a soupy concoction made of coconut milk, tapioca beads, small squares of coconut gel, and pink pieces of watermelon. A fruity, soothing, tropical flavor that was refreshing in the humid summer air. The perfect dessert.

Without prompting Junichi stood up and put a ladle into the melon. He filled a small dessert bowl with white liquid and passed it on to us. Throughout our trip I had observed that serving was a task delegated to women. When we commented on how helpful Junichi was, his wife Takako reported that when her sister Hajime and Hisakazu were first married, Hajime would complain that she had no help with the household chores. She would then hold up Junichi as exemplary husband. Hajime's lament, of course, was "Why aren't you more like Junichi!" To which Hisakazu had predictably replied, "If you wanted a man like him, you should have married Junichi!" Nevertheless, in some Japanese households there appeared to be a little measure of equality. But no woman raised in Japan would ever jump over a chair to be the first in line to paint pottery. Too bold!

Monday, 30th of June 1997
Hamaoka's/ Yanagawa City and a Singing Gondolier/ Nagasu Onsen

I rose early and showered, dressed and went across the street to a convenience store for a bottle of water and *nigiri*, rice shaped into a small ball, with which I could take with my medicine. When I got back to the room, Diane was up and had turned on the television. On the screen, British troops dressed in red uniforms paraded through the streets of Hong Kong. Drums were beating and trumpets blaring. I turned up the volume to find out what all the hoopla was about.

The British were officially turning over the governance of Hong Kong to China, and the ceremony marked the end of the "Ninety-Nine-Years Lease." The event was observed with a great deal of pomp and circumstance, the likes of which I had not seen since the coronation of Queen Elizabeth II in 1952.

The reportage was clearly appropriate for the significance of the event, but I wondered if it was being given the same attention by the U.S. East Coast media. It was my perception that papers like the *New York Times* and *Washington Post* tended to be dim in their coverage of Asian events. I could not ponder the question for long because the Hamaoka's, Mom's father's family, were coming to collect us.

Diane and I went down to the lobby. Mom and the rest of our party were already there and the Iwatas had come to the hotel to see us off. All together we took over half of the lobby for more group pictures. The young men seemed more relaxed today and kidded around with each other. I thanked Mr. Iwata and said my good-bys. I was feeling particularly grateful. My family has and will undoubtedly continue to play host to them when they visit California, but since I live in New York, it is doubtful that I will ever be able to reciprocate their kindness. Hisakazu has been the link for both families, and we were richer for his efforts.

As was the case earlier in our tour, a private van arrived at the hotel. Although the driver wore white gloves, as had professional drivers before him, the driver of this van was our distant cousin. Shinichi Hamaoka, my grandfather's great-nephew had rented a van and ridden with his brother-in-law driver to take us home where his family was hosting lunch. We piled our luggage into the van, said our final "Good-by, come and see us in America…" to the Iwatas and got in.

It was roasting inside. The windows were shut and the men had been smoking. I thought, "We ain't gonna make it. We'll faint first." Mom came to the rescue. She asked the men to turn on the air conditioner, and when they looked befuddled, guided them through the process. They thanked her and explained they had never operated a van before.

A half hour later after a comfortable ride on a modern highway, we pulled up in front of the offices of the Hamaoka Construction Company, Shinichi's place of business. Shinichi and Mom went in while we waited outside. At the top of the modern two-story building alongside *kanji* characters the name Hamaoka was printed in *rōmánji* or English letters.

> *One summer, Dad took GT and me for a ride along the Sacramento River. We drove along a narrow two-lane road that wound around the delta. Dad knew every levee and slough on the delta and could narrate countless stories. At one point, we crossed the water on a ferry: a platform big enough for two cars. "One night Mr....drove down here. It was dark, he missed the ferry, drove into the river and drowned," Dad recounted. Above us at the entrance to a drawbridge was a gatehouse, and Dad waved at the gatemaster who waved back. "After the war when we came back from the camps, it was hard to find jobs and there was still a lot of prejudice against Japanese. Mr....got a job operating the drawbridge. Then the State took over, and he got State pay and good benefits," he reported. We ended up in Walnut Grove, the small town where Dad had spent his childhood. At the end of an unpaved road stood a warehouse with "Inaba-Co 1936 [sic]" etched above the doorway. Dad stood beneath the sign, and I took a picture.*

I grabbed the nearest models, Stephanie and Robyn, made them stand beneath the Hamaoka sign and snapped a photo. The Hamaoka Construction Company appeared to be a mid-size family owned and run business, much like those enterprises run by the Inaba Brothers in the States. I think had the Hamaokas and Inabas stayed in Japan, Mom and Dad would have still ended up married to each other.

A large assortment of great-aunts and second, third, and fourth cousins were assembled for lunch at Shinichi's house. *Ji-chan* Hamaoka was the sixth sibling in a family of eight. Shinichi's grandfather was number seven, and number eight was a brother who had gone to America with *Ji-chan*. All of the Hamaoka's present at lunch represented the offspring of those brothers. There were only five males in the lunch party that numbered a total of twenty-four.

One of our great-aunts was holding Shinichi's baby grandson in her arms. This baby was passed from one set of arms to another, and was as comfortable with each aunt or cousin who held him as they were with him. Taka-chan, another of Shinichi's grandsons, came racing through the rooms. He was four years old, wore an "Ultra-Man" t-shirt, and clearly distressed. He pulled his mother along, and cried, *"Damé, damé, damé!"* afraid that we were going to touch the toys stacked up at one end of the room. Despite his mother's attempts, he would not be mollified. He finally calmed down after one of his aunts stepped in.

Child rearing activities were shared by all of the Hamaoka women. When we were growing up in Fresno, sometimes our cousins would come over on a Sunday afternoon. My poor grandmother was in charge of nine or ten children while our parents worked. Those Sunday afternoons were the closest experience I personally had to that type of an extended family. Like many American families, we are pretty much spread out over the country and Asia is lucky when she is able to see her cousins once a year.

Our hosts had prepared a feast in our honor. Every inch of two low tables was covered with platters and dishes. Mom sat like royalty between Shinichi and his son, who had come home from the office to join us. Across from her sat her cousins Sadame and Sadako, two sisters who spent part their childhood in American.

> The year that Dad died, Mom flew to the East Coast to tour colleges for Asia with us. It was a bittersweet time for her, happy that Asia was a candidate for some major Ivy League campuses, but sad that Dad was not around to share this with us. We ended up in Providence, Rhode Island. GT took the train back to the city because he had to work, and Mom and I shared a room at the Holiday Inn. We had settled in for the night, and in that very private quiet time, Mom recounted this story: "I was little and we were living in Delano. Ji-chan's brother and his wife were moving back to Japan. They had two girls, my cousins, who were a little older than me. We went to see them off at the place where they were getting on the ship, and one of my cousins was wearing a red hat with a fringe on it. I looked at that hat, and I looked at it. And finally I said, 'Where did you get that hat?' And she said, 'Oh, you want it?' I nodded, and she took it off and put it on my head."

I wondered if Sadako the red-hat cousin remembered her spontaneous gift of kindness and generosity that stayed with Mom all these years. Mom asked her, but she had no recollection of the occurrence.

I sat next to Shinichi's sister Fukumi who told me that she had been to New York City. She said she was able to get around easily, but felt there was a lot more than the parts of Manhattan to which she was exposed. Her daughter had also been to New York and had ridden the subway from her hotel in Midtown to the Blue Note jazz club in Greenwich Village. I was impressed. I couldn't imagine doing something like that in Tokyo by myself at night.

Fukumi announced that she and another cousin Kiyoko would take us to see some of the local sights. They planned to take us to Yanagawa where we would take a ride on a…Fukumi said something that I didn't understand. We did a verbal back-and-forth, and she unmistakably said "Venice." "Venice?" I asked. She explained that Yanagawa is the Venice of Japan. Then I got the word she had been saying, *gondola*. We would take a gondola ride. Mom was comfortable and begged off joining us so that she could spend time resting and visiting with her cousins.

Our tour guides for the day, Fukumi and Kiyoko led us up a winding sidewalk next to a canal and onto a dock with a wooden boathouse. Posters advertised gondola rides in seasonal splendors: under branches thick with cherry blossoms in one picture, and red-orange maple leaves in another, straw-hatted gondoliers pushed on their poles at the sterns of their boats.

Fukumi purchased tickets and we headed onto the dock. It was a hot hazy day, and a half-dozen boats were moored to the pier. A boatman wearing a straw coolie hat and short *hapi* coat greeted us as we boarded his open gondola.

Informing the boatman that we were from America, Fukumi asked if he might sing us a song. Feigning modesty, he said his voice was not good enough for *musume-san*, or young ladies. Fukumi responded in the expected Japanese manner, and politely asked him again to please sing for us. They bandied back-and-forth while he pushed away from the dock.

We glided along the narrow canal. At that point in the ride, backs of buildings lined the bank and the boatman pointed out a wall painted white and explained that we were going by the birthplace and home of Hakushu Kitahara, a famous writer and poet.

The boatman ducked his head to get under a bridge, the lowest one on the canal. We moved downstream, making slow, curving turns. Both sides of the banks were lush with trees and leafy plants. Small docks intruded at different intervals, and the boatman identified a wedding dock where a bride and her family boarded a gondola on her wedding day. Apparently, on some days it was customary to see many brides in *tsunokakushi* or traditional bridal hats sitting proudly at the bows of the boats.

The ride seemed effortless. We passed under the shade of huge trees and weeping willows that grew down to the water. We floated under arched pedestrian bridges, which crossed the canal. Only one other boat glided ahead of us, and we felt as though we had the river to ourselves.

Our boatman began to sing. He had a strong tenor voice. I could not catch the meaning of the words but the melody was pleasing and went with the mood of the ride.

Lovely ladies glide,
River winds through soothing song,
Summer serenade.

At the end of our ride, we thanked the man and disembarked. We walked in front of the buildings that bordered the canal. Fukumi pointed out a house with a white lattice fence, and informed us that we had earlier floated by the back of this home belonging to the poet Hakushu Kitahara. I did not know the poet or his work, but the locals gave him such respect that we pulled out our cameras and posed for pictures.

We walked down the sloping street to a Victorian-looking building with pillars and a front porch. Fukumi announced that we were entering the Ohana Villa. The villa was part of the estate of the local ruling lord, and reportedly built during the Meiji era. It had been preserved and opened to the public as a museum. One of the rooms inside looked exactly like the set out of the Takaraduka play we had seen earlier on our tour. It seemed everywhere we went, we bumped into references to the Meiji era, a distinct turning point in Japanese history.

We entered the Shoten Garden, which featured a large pond with rocks and pine trees, and posed for more pictures. Perhaps if we had been here earlier in our trip, it would have been more memorable. But alas! Japanese Gardens were going the way of Shinto shrines and Buddhist temples, and I could not tell one garden from another. It was getting late, we were getting tired, and it was time to go.

For our last night in Japan, Cousin Shinichi had arranged for us to stay at the Nagasu Inn. Our accommodations were traditional: fold-out futons on the floor and the *ofuro* or bath at the end of the hall. We were five to a room, the girls claimed one of the rooms and took their Auntie Lynne with them, and the rest of us adults took the other.

I went to relax in the hot *ofuro* before dinner, and then joined the rest of our party in our private dining room. Dinner was also traditionally Japanese and I am sure it was delicious, but at that point I would have given my right arm and all of my toes for a slice of thin crust New York pizza.

Diane discovered the gastronomical treat of the meal. "Ummm," she said dipping her chopsticks into a small plate, "Stewed prunes. Leslee, taste the prunes. These prunes are to die for!" "Do you hear yourself?" Asia asked. "You're turning into such an old lady!"

We learned that guests had come to see us and after our hostess cleared the table, she ushered them in the room. More relatives. At least a dozen of them clustered together sitting on their knees in the far corner of the room, while we received them like ladies of a court. The scene was so Japanese: a trace of feudalism, a strict code of class-based propriety, and a sense of simple courtesy. Our guests did not stay long. We said our goodnights and retired to our rooms.

Everyone did her last-minute packing. We had given out all the *omiyage* we brought with us, but had a good amount of items to take back. We used all of the pockets and corners of our suitcases, and stored our luggage in one end of the room for easy collection in the morning. Not everyone was ready to fall asleep, but Mom called lights out and before my head hit the pillow, snores rumbled from several futons in the room.

Tuesday, 1st of July 1997 (The Forty-One Hour Day)
Kumamoto to Fukuoka to Tokyo to San Francisco

Fourteen days in Japan and we had become veteran travelers. No wake-up calls for us. With military discipline, we along with our luggage were ready to roll when a van and a car full of Hamaokas pulled up. Our hosts Shinichi and Takeko, and Fukumi and Kiyoko from the boat ride, and little Taka-chan, his mother, and two other children spilled out of the vehicles. We gathered on the steps at the entrance to the inn for what had become the customary group photographs, grateful thank-yous, and wistful good-bys.

The first leg of our trip home was an hour-and-a-half plane ride from Fukuoka to Haneda airport in Tokyo. As we checked our bags at the airport, Lynne pulled out the toy gun she had bought in Osaka. The security guard was startled. Lynne said, "*Omócha, watashi no kodomo*," literally translated, "Toy, my child," and waved the receipt at him. Amazingly (and alarmingly) he let her through with the gun, although he did confiscate the air canister.

We were practically the only passengers on a major aircraft with a full crew. I was assigned to an aisle seat but got up and moved next to the window. The flight attendant looked at me as if she wanted me to stay in my assigned place, but in the big empty plane, as the phrase goes, "I don't think so." I thought of the money it must cost Japan Air Lines to make the flight. So much waste. I wondered how they could stay in business, and then I remembered that JAL enjoys substantial government subsidies.

When we landed at Haneda airport, Hisakazu Iwata was there to meet us. He escorted us as we traveled by bus to Narita Airport where Katsuyuki and Junko (our hosts from Kyoto) were waiting to see us off. The Iwatas had come full circle with us, present at our arrival and there at our departure. They helped us organize our luggage and walked us over to the check in counter. After much prodding, Mom convinced them that we would be all right and they reluctantly took their leave.

Security was tighter flying out of Narita than in Fukuoka. At the check in counter, passengers were made to open their luggage for a thorough search by security guards. Stephanie was in line behind me, and as our turns approached, she began to fidget. She sifted from one leg to the next like a little kid who needed to go to the bathroom. Finally, she exclaimed aloud, "Okay, okay!" and pulled some sparkler-type fireworks out of her suitcase. She was going to try to sneak them through. No one had called her on anything; it was just her conscience and the fear of getting caught that made her confess. Her mother reprimanded her, but I was just glad she had a conscience.

Our flight did not leave until six o'clock in the evening. We had hours of downtime and the energy level of ten deflated balloons. We wandered through a shopping arcade and picked over the merchandise. Cindy and Diane bought a key chain that sang, "*Cha-ka, Cha-ka,*" and gave it to Asia as a final souvenir.

I plopped down on a seat and surveyed the waiting area. Our group was assembled in small clusters of two and threes across the room from each other. A mood of subtle edginess had settled in. Two weeks together on our best behavior was beginning to strain and with only hours to go, minor annoyances that lurked beneath the surface threatened to erupt like pimples on a teenager's face. Instinctively, we drew into our corners and kept respectful distances.

I expected the upper deck seating arrangements we had on our flight out and was disappointed when we finally boarded the aircraft and found our assigned seats in the last row before the smoking section. Seated behind us, some men from China were traveling to America for the first time. I knew that they were from China because they wore gray 1950's style suits, spoke Mandarin, and smoked strong cigarettes. I knew they were traveling to the U.S. for the first time because they generated the same anticipatory energy as did we when we flew out of San Francisco fourteen days earlier.

I was not accustomed to cigarette smoke. I felt queasy as my stomach sent waves of bile up my esophagus. If it had just been nausea, I would have treated myself with some club soda. But my symptoms were layered under exhaustion and secondhand smoke. I just wanted to sleep, and ordered wine with my meal hoping it would help. Wrong choice. The wine revved up the churning in my stomach. I grabbed my in-flight sick bag and made a beeline for the bathroom. Once I upchucked, I was good for the rest of the trip.

We traveled thousands of miles in the air, crossed some invisible time line, and at eleven o'clock in the morning on the same day and seven hours before we had taken off in Tokyo, we landed in San Francisco. We bounced out of the aircraft with renewed energy, happy to be home. Mom was relieved that we were all back in one piece with no accidents, illnesses, or incidents. Adventurous anticipation was replaced by successful completion.

Darryl, Harley and Dan were waiting for us outside of customs. Diane, Cindy and Stephanie were bursting with stories for Darryl. Harley gathered up Judy and Robyn, eager to be with his girls again. Observing the reunion between her Aunt Sharon and Uncle Dan, Asia had an interesting comment. "Mom, it's all there." she exclaimed. "Uncle Danny will always be Auntie Sharon's teenage heartthrob!"

Lynne was summoned home the minute we landed. There seemed to have been an emergency of sorts, and she had to drive three hours to Fresno. I felt badly for her. She did not get even an hour to decompress.

Asia and I rode with Darryl and his family to their house. Nibbles the fat cat was sitting next to the stove in front of his feeding dish as though he had been there the entire time we were gone. He did not even get up and run away like he usually did. He must have missed the girls (or perhaps he had gotten so fat that he just could not walk anymore).

I called GT and told him we were back. Asia and I would stay the night in San Francisco, and then we would catch the redeye to New York.

Wednesday, 2ⁿᵈ of July and Thursday, 3ʳᵈ of July 1997
San Francisco to New York

I heard the motor open and close the garage door, and felt the ever-present dampness that is San Francisco before I opened my eyes. Darryl must have gone off to work. I listened for creaking sounds of anyone who was awake and moving upstairs, but heard none. It was eight o'clock in the morning. I did the math in my head. Eight in the morning in San Francisco made eleven in the morning in New York. Okay, so I should get up. But it was midnight in Tokyo. Midnight tomorrow. So, should I stay in bed? I could not fuss with it any longer. I needed to do some laundry—not much, just the clothes that were damp and seemingly beginning to grow mildew. But before that, I needed to get out and exercise. I pulled on my running gear, slipped out the front door, and headed for the beach.

The day was overcast but clear patches of blue were beginning to break through the clouds. I headed toward Sloat and then down toward the ocean. I promised myself that I would take the same route coming back.

Mingled scents of eucalyptus and pine were welcoming and familiar. Pastel-painted houses had a bigness to them, and the streets seemed extraordinarily wide. Nothing had changed in the two weeks I was gone, but it had all changed. My perceptions had changed.

The incessant roar of the ocean announced its presence before it appeared—yards of blue fabric stretched across the horizon. Next to the shoreline, cars raced along the Great Highway. I caught a traffic light, crossed the highway to the sandy bluffs above the beach, and stared to jog. Cars zipped along to my right, and to my left the ocean expanded westward. Somewhere far beyond the horizon, all those commuters I saw on the busy streets of Osaka and Hiroshima had scurried home. They had their dinners and were tucked into their futons enjoying a restful night's sleep. I could not see them, but I knew they were there. I was there yesterday, when it was today.

Close to ninety-years ago, *Ji-chan* Inaba crossed that ocean, and then *Ba-chan* Inaba followed him. *Ji-chan* Hamaoka came over with his brother and his family. They all came to seek their fortunes, and I suspect they meant to go back to Japan for a life of leisure once they had done so. *Ba-chan* Hamaoka made the voyage by herself to marry a husband she had never met. It took over a month by ship. More than thirty days for what we had done in nine hours.

I once asked Ba-chan Hamaoka why she had come to America. She was staying with Auntie Hisa in San Francisco and I was a teacher in Berkeley. It was in the declining years of her life after she had a series of minor strokes, and she was growing frail. I wanted to spend some time with her, so I arranged to pick her up one Friday evening. She would spend the night with me and I had planned to take her to the rose garden at Lake Merritt Park in Oakland the next day.

I was twenty-four at the time and totally involved in my work. After I collected Ba-chan and brought her home, I got a phone call about some kind of project that needed to be done and ended up working most of the next morning. It wasn't until late in the afternoon that I finally drove Ba-chan to the park.

We walked along a curving sidewalk next to the lake. I knew the entrance to the rose garden was somewhere ahead of us, but I didn't know how much farther we had to go. We passed clumps of ordinary, but colorful, blossoming flowers. Ba-chan was tiring, so we found a bench on which to rest. She had shrunken and was so little that her feet didn't touch the ground. Her legs swung freely, like those of little children their first day of kindergarten. We sat there, the two of us, on a park bench in the late afternoon sun.

"Ba-chan, A-me-ri-ca ni na-shi-te ki-ma-shi-ta?" I asked. "Why did you come to America?" She laughed, putting her hand over her mouth. "Ame-ri-ka mo mi-tai-to o-motta," she said. It was just that simple. "I came to American because I thought I'd like to check it out." And she was off on her adventure.

We never did find the rose garden. I drove her back to San Francisco, and later that day Auntie Hisa called to thank me for taking Ba-chan out. She said Ba-chan told her she had never seen such beautiful flowers.

Knowing what I know about the chapters in *Ba-chan's* life, I wondered how many times she might have regretted her decision to come to America. The year our family drove to the site of the Amache Internment Camp, she refused to go with us. When I asked her about it, she had tears in her eyes and said in effect, "Why would anyone want to go there?"

Yet, she lived to see the good times. The fortunes that were made and the opportunities that were realized. She would have been elated about her eldest daughter taking her granddaughters and granddaughters-in-law and great-granddaughters on a pilgrimage of sorts to meet their relatives and absorb the place where she grew up.

I think we all made some kind of a connection. My links came in the late afternoon haze at Ise Bay overlooking the Meoto Iwa rocks, and in the magic of the Inaba homestead. Those experiences let me know that I was connected to Japan in ways I had never imagined. Yet, I am too much my own person to live in Japan. In connecting to Japan, I realized my own American-ness.

The sun had broken into the patchy sky, and the morning was brilliant as only it can be on a clear San Francisco summer day. The Pacific Ocean rolled to my west as I jogged on top of the sand dunes along the Great Highway.

I blessed Ba-chan for having had the courage to cross that ocean.

Looking back over the last two weeks, it was clear that we were wined and dined like royalty. The trip was a luxury built on three generations of sacrifice and hard work.

The girls were perhaps a little young to realize the value of what they had experienced, but I hoped someday they would come to appreciate what their grandmother had provided for them. I suspected that they would, in their own time and fashion. After all, they come from a long line of strong women.

I reached the traffic light at the foot of Sloat and stretched my legs over a fence post on the side of the jogging path. It was time to head back to Darryl's. In less than twelve hours, Asia and I would be boarding our flight to New York, the last leg of our trip home.

EPILOGUE

Asia and I landed at JFK at six o'clock the morning of the 3rd of July and took a cab back to our apartment. I unlocked our front door, and GT came padding from the bedroom in his bare feet. He hugged us, "Glad you're back." We were glad to be back.

I spent the day unpacking, doing laundry, and sorting out the gifts that we had brought back. GT had stacked old newspapers to throw out, and on the top of the pile was the July 1st issue of the *New York Times*. Banner headlines announced the return of Hong Kong to China and pictured the same British troops in red uniforms that I had seen on television in Japan. Front-page news was front-page news regardless of where one is in the world, after all. That was reassuring.

Somewhere in the early afternoon, time caught up with me. I crashed for a couple of hours and awoke around dinnertime to the aroma of GT's special enchilada sauce simmering on the stove.

I had one last holiday before my everyday-routine reclaimed my life. July 4th, Independence Day. Asia left the apartment in the early morning, eager to meet up with her friends. GT and I spent the day relaxing and viewing from our apartment window the parade of picnic-goers—shopping carts full of beer and soda, franks and chicken, charcoal and portable barbecues—on a continuous march to the East River Park.

That evening through our bedroom window we watched fireworks launched from barges on the East River fill the sky and sparkle over the Brooklyn and Manhattan Bridges.

> *Glitter explodes red,*
> *Then white, blue. Their pops and bangs*
> *Announce: Welcome home!*

978-0-595-37496-0
0-595-37496-4